AIRPORT MARKETING

To baby Sofia, my greatest joy

Airport Marketing

Strategies to Cope with the New Millennium Environment

DAVID JARACH
SDA Bocconi Graduate School of Business, Italy

ASHGATE

Published by
Ashgate Publishing Limited
Gower House
Croft Road
Aldershot
Hampshire GU11 3HR
England

Ashgate Publishing Company
Suite 420
101 Cherry Street
Burlington, VT 05401-4405
USA

Ashgate website: http://www.ashgate.com

British Library Cataloguing in Publication Data
Jarach, David
    Airport marketing : strategies to cope with the new
    millennium environment
    1.Airports - Marketing 2.Airports - Economic aspects
    I.Title
    387.7'364'0688

Library of Congress Cataloging-in-Publication Data
Jarach, David.
    Airport marketing : strategies to cope with the new millennium environment / by
David Jarach.
        p. cm.
    Includes bibliographical references and index.
    ISBN 0-7546-4085-X
    1. Airports--Economic aspects. 2. Airports--Management. 3. Aeronautics,
Commercial--Economic aspects. I. Title.

    HE9797.4.E3J37 2005
    387.7'36'0688--dc22

                                                                2005011793

ISBN-10: 0 7546 4085 X
ISBN-13: 978 0 7546 4085 1

Reprinted 2006

Printed and bound in Great Britain by MPG Books Ltd, Bodmin, Cornwall

Contents

List of Tables

List of Figures

Acknowledgements

Initially, I would like to extend my warmest thanks to Professor Enrico Valdani for the sincere, close and effective support he has given me since I started out in academia.

I also thank Bruno Busacca and Sandro Castaldo, former and current director of the Marketing Department at SDA Bocconi, for their long-lasting support in developing executive programs tailored to the needs of the air transport pipeline. Thanks also to all my colleagues at SDA Bocconi's Marketing Department, a beautiful environment based on the values of friendship and mutual support. In particular thanks to my colleague and friend Eleonora Cattaneo for supporting me during the revision of this book.

I thank my friends Jacques Tournut and Sveinn Gudmundsson for the experience of being Visiting Professor at Toulouse Business School, Aerospace MBA, a stimulating environment to extend knowledge frontiers.

Thanks to Julian Peinador, Vice-Dean at ESIC Business School at Madrid for hosting me as Visiting Professor and for sharing refreshing new ideas with me concerning the world of executive education on a pan European basis.

I also thank all friends at the Air Transport Research Society (ATRS). I was honoured to join the Association and later to be co-opted into its prestigious World Network Committee. I thank especially: Tae Oum, Brent Bowen and Respicio A. Espirito Santo, Jr.

I am grateful to my publisher, John Hindley. *Grazie mille*, John, for your wonderful patience and for the never-ending encouragement given during all the writing and publication phases of this book. Thanks also to Pauline Beavers, my desk editor, for the help she has given in achieving the goal of a well edited book. Special thanks to Jacinta McDonnell from DKM Economic Consultants, who also supported me in the editing phase of this book.

My thanks to all managers that have participated for almost a decade in my executive courses entitled 'Marketing for the air transport business' at SDA Bocconi. This book is also a product of many class-discussions and dinners with some of them.

I am also grateful to all chairmen, CEOs, managers and executives of the air transport pipeline who have shared their experiences for years during my consulting and advisory activities. This interaction permitted me to put into practice, and continually fine-tune, my industry expertise.

Thanks to Mark Pilling of the prestigious *Airline Business* monthly magazine, for his interest in my ideas when dealing with air transport scenarios in the Italian context. For the same reason, thanks to Igino Coggi, editor in chief of *Air Press*, the Italian point of reference for aviation, to Gianfranco Fabi and Gianni Dragoni, deputy editor-in-chief and a reporter from *Sole24Ore*, the main Italian economic newspaper and to Simonetta Scarane and Sabina Rodi of the economic daily *Italia Oggi*.

Finally, I thank my family, the real source of energy and enthusiasm behind my work. Thanks to my father, Daniel, and my mother, Annamaria, for all the love they have given and continue to give. And, especially, thanks to my wife Elena for her love and for the patience she has shown over all the time I denied her, in writing articles and books, this one included, and, more generally, when dealing with aviation topics and practices. And lastly, a wonderful welcome to our baby girl Sofia, to whom this book is dedicated: I love you, *bimbotta*.

David Jarach
Milan, Italy

Preface

Royal/Dutch Shell is one of the world's premier oil companies, with a history dating back to when the same oil industry was born. Shell was market leader for many years in the UK, one of its home markets. However, in a relatively short amount of time, Shell's comfort zone was successfully attacked and taken over by an innovative value proposition. As such, Shell's top managers realised that a supermarket chain, Tesco, had become the largest petrol retailer in Britain.

Similarly, we may think of current trends in the banking business. Monopolistic or oligopolistic rents have been destroyed firstly by national deregulation; and then, traditional banking propositions have been hit by a technological 'quantum leap' driven by the upsurge of on-line banks. Customers have already experienced some consequences of this evolved market scenario: an increased range of value-driven competition, a continuous development of new marketing tools to attract and retain customers and, eventually, some consolidation practices between players to get economies of costs from both internal and external processes.

In a broader sense, the continued disruption of once stable arenas permits unexpected competitors to emerge thanks to technological changes, globalisation and deregulation patterns, the constitution of new clusters of demanding customers rather than the availability of parallel, unlocked distribution channels. Firms with little respect for industry conventions are thus able to overcome the existing boundaries, establish new patterns of interactions and eventually experiment with sound economic returns even in sufficiently difficult times.

Hyper competition, turbo competition or simply 'unexpected competition', due to convergence of apparently separate and discordant industries to form 'meta-markets', therefore puts managers in a position to look for a radical shift in their strategic market approach.

First of all, they must have a deep understanding of both the magnitude and the diversity of the various forms of competition by using advanced tools and methodologies to avoid marginalisation in their own core business. In other words, they have to improve their in-depth knowledge about the enlarged ecologic system in which their company lives.

Second, managers have to keep in mind that innovation in business concepts and designs is much more than a simple imperative, if their companies want to maintain a positioning at the forefront of the profit continuum and, thus, get extra revenues and yields from the market. The goal of business concept innovation is to introduce more strategic variety into an industry or competitive domain. When this happens, and when customers value positively this proposition, the distribution of wealth-creating potential may dramatically shift in favour of the innovator.

Turning our attention to airport practices, evidence clearly shows that value has increasingly migrated away from traditional business designs tailored to serve airlines' needs towards new business designs that better match the shifting priorities both of current and of new clusters of end customers.

Thus, airports whose aims are to reach a status of 'best-in-class operators' must generate new incremental commercial experiences that reinforce their power of attraction to both passenger and cargo businesses. Airports must also project enlarged value designs to capture, in a new platform of consumption, airports' neighbouring residents, meeters and greeters, airport employees, air transport employees and, eventually, companies located within the airport's catchment area.

This market-based rather than innovative 'quantum leap' approach is being implemented by a new category of airports entering the market arena: the so-called 'commercial airports'. These players strive to perform an extreme diversification of 'non-aviation related' activities within its own boundaries, instead that conserving a sole and conservative focus on 'aviation-related' services. This shift is not simply a consequence of a narcissistic will to improve airports' appeal, but a current economic need to fight the downward spiral that is cutting margins on former traditional sources of monopolistic rent for airport authorities. Thus, in a short amount of time, airports that have not undergone a transition from old to this new value design will be almost certainly marginalised and can only survive in a subsidised environment.

This book aims first to explore the existing boundaries of the airport industry within the air transport value chain. The basic economics of the airport business will be examined and a correlation analysis of B2B and B2C relationships within the air transport value chain will take place.

Furthermore, the two main strategic business units (SBUs) of modern airport enterprises, the 'aviation-related' and the 'non-aviation related' ones, will be explored by using a new line of research and a creative paradigm of analysis. The use of a significant number of micro-cases will support the analysis as appropriate. Following the presentation of some new ideas, like the launch of Airport Loyalty Programs, a description of the main steps of an airport marketing plan will also be provided.

The final part of the book will be dealing with security issues that the industry is facing within the post-September 11 scenario. Some of the answers that international ruling bodies are now trying to put in practice to reduce the terrorist threat will be described and analysed. These pages have been written together with Mr. Alfredo Roma, a former chairman of ENAC (The Italian Civil Aviation Authority) and current ECAC (European Civil Aviation Conference) president and, due to this double role, certainly one of most involved people in exploring security solutions for the industry since the early moments after the Twin Towers' attack.

After a presentation of some data on the airport business in 2002, 2003 and 2004, this book, finally, hosts a postface signed by Mr. Jean Cyril Spinetta, Chairman of Air France. These pages are aimed at showing the perspective of a mega carrier on the evolution of the market relationship with airports in the New Millennium environment.

List of Abbreviations

ACI	Airport Council International
ALP	Airport Loyalty Program
ASA	Air Service Agreements
B2B	Business to Business
B2C	Business to Consumer
B2T	Business to Trade
BAA	British Airport Authority
CLTV	Customer Lifetime Value
ECAC	European Civil Aviation Conference
EDS	Explosive Detection System
ENAC	Ente Nazionale Aviazione Civile (Italian Civil Aviation Authority)
FAA	Federal Aviation Administration
FFP	Frequent Flyer Program
GSA	General Sales Agent
IATA	International Air Transport Association
ICAO	International Civil Aviation Organisation
KPI	Key Performance Index
LCA	London City Airport
MCT	Minimum Check-in Time
MSSP	Marketing Support System Plan
SBU	Strategic Business Unit
VFR	Visiting Friends and Relatives

Chapter 1

The Airport Enterprise: Role and Scope of Activity

The Role and Scope of Activity of the Airport Enterprise

Airports are an essential part of the air transport system. They play a vital role not only within the macro environment of transportation, but also in the process of increasing the quality of life of their regional economies directly participating in wealth creation. They can thus be considered as leading players in regards to economic, productive, tourist and commercial upgrades of a territory, thanks to the 'multiplier effect' in the number of potential business transactions they may stimulate.

As a logical consequence of this, it seems narrow-minded to associate too closely airports with the concept of aerodromes, where historically aircraft simply landed and were parked. On the contrary, airports encompass a number of operational and commercial processes, with inherent complexities in their management and coordination phases. This seems truer in the current situation of increasing environmental turbulence and broadening competitive pressures.

We may, thus, look at airports as real *enterprises*, their goal being long-term profit generation that can both sustain independent development and reward stakeholders. We can further break down the current mission of *airport-enterprises* within five highly correlated pillars of action.

The Economic Impact on Countries and Regions

Scheduled and chartered air transportation provides a significant impact on the economy of the region it serves, involving both the inhabitants and local businesses.

The extent of the benefit depends on the mix of traffic (business vs. tourist), the type of scheduled service (domestic vs. international, long-haul vs. short-haul, point-to-point vs. hub-and-spoke), the magnitude and origin of charter operations, the relative isolation of the region and the availability of other modes of transportation. For example, a single non-stop daily flight with a 200-seat wide-body aircraft between a mid-size city in the USA and a major city in Western Europe (say, London) is expected to contribute a couple of hundred million dollars per year to the economy of the region (Taneja, 2003).

The Logistical and Infrastructural Dimension

Airports assure significant logistic support in the movement of both short, medium and long-haul passengers and goods to and from a specific geographic area, acting as gateways of inbound and outbound business and tourist traffic for a territory.

A superior capacity, a qualified package of support infrastructures and effective managerial practice will be key elements in the improvement of competitive capabilities of local actors, too.

The Hub Dimension in the 'Marketing of Places' Perspective

Airports also play a strategic role for the regions they serve, as they may accelerate the pace of growth of a territory's visibility on the world map. An airport's distinctive positioning may become a primary asset in the attraction of new manufacturing activities in certain geographic areas and, thus, a significant driver in the development of the territory's value proposition. In fact, transport infrastructures are primarily evaluated by multinationals in the case of international development of activities because of their direct impact on logistic efficiency and effectiveness.

Airports, in other words, may permit companies to successfully exploit both local comparative advantages and reinforce the firm's own international competitive supremacy. Whilst, for the regional territory, airports are able to improve the rate of employment of local residents by means of third-party[1] new job creation.

The Marketing Dimension of Airport Enterprises in the Air Transport Value Chain

In parallel with historical B2B links within the pipeline with airlines, travel agents, tour operators, catering arms, car rentals, air charter brokers and GSAs, airports are developing new innovative market strategies to contact end-customers and then directly manage long-term relationships with them.

---

[1] Jobs are created by the opening of new greenfield industrial plants in the airport's catchment area.

Chapter 2 will explain in detail the air transport value chain's main business links.

The Political Value of Airport Enterprises

Airports are also used by political bodies as a fundamental tool in the practice of establishing and reinforcing citizens' consensus.

First, building airport infrastructures requires major financial and human resources, with a positive economic spillover to local macroeconomic figures. For instance, airport services, like handling, are typically labour-intensive activities, with major opportunities for directly creating new jobs for nearby communities. Moreover, the opening or upgrading of a terminal complex may be perceived as an economic benefit by some related businesses, like hotels, restaurants, ground transportation, and so on. Eventually, the opening of an airport usually requires investments in ground accessibility in terms of an enriched package of motorway and railways connections.

All these elements may be considered as positive externalities that in some way balance negative issues such as those concerning environmental pollution generated by aircraft movements.

Fund-Raising Activity and the Main Governance Patterns in the Airport Business

The nature of public-sector intervention in supporting airport development may be examined from two different perspectives:

- financing and fund raising activities, in the case of either greenfield building or simpler terminal expansion;
- a governance activity, dealing with fixing ownership and conduct rules for each airport enterprise.

Financing and Fund-Raising Phase

Most of the world's airports lie on land directly owned by the state, which explains why virtually all airports were traditionally owned by the public sector.

For instance, European airports serving major cities such as Paris, London, Dublin, Stockholm, Copenhagen, Madrid and Geneva were all owned by national governments, as were many other airports outside

Europe, such as those in Tokyo, Singapore, Bangkok, Sydney and Johannesburg. Elsewhere, local governments, either at a regional or municipal level, were the airport owners, as in the US (Graham, 2001).

As a result, the public sector has thus historically been awarded the responsibility of being the main generator of cash resources in planning and building airports, within a primary goal of enriching the infrastructural package of the country.

The role of States as the main financial sponsors of the airport business seems today, however, to be under serious threat by a combination of significant factors. The first one is related to the magnitude of investments in this industry that have already been scheduled for the years to come. Recent ICAO figures show that up until 2005, 250 to 300 billion USD will be invested in the creation of new platforms or in the expansion of current ones. The second one is linked to cost-cutting measures that have been heavily hitting State budgets for the last decade. These measures are related to the stabilisation of economies within integrated currency areas, such as in the case of Euro land,[2] or, in a broader sense, to reduce the burden of State debt which has its own negative effects on private investments.

In this evolving scenario, new techniques of fund-raising are being scrutinised with increasing attention, like in the case of project-financing and, thus, direct involvement of private companies in this activity. Self-financing by individual airports appears to be rather difficult, primarily due to the magnitude of resources needed for it.

Governance Phase

According to a systemic governance view, central authorities act in supervising, checking and regulating airport enterprises' conducts. This task finds a visible implementation in the designation of proprietary rules to apply for each airport, this implying the type and quality of its shareholders, too.

In this sense, we may find four different types of governance practices for airports, each one with a different mix of private and public actors involved:

---

[2]The Maastricht Treaty requires Member States to respect certain macro-parameters that limit their freedom in the area of financing public expenditure.

- direct government control. This occurs when a central government agency (frequently named Civil Aviation Authority[3]) is awarded the responsibility to manage the country's aviation practices: this is what happens in Greece, Sweden and Norway. This control, in the case of a federal entity, for instance, may also be delegated to regions and their own dedicated departments;
- decentralised public control through airport authorities. Some governments and municipalities have passed over their governance powers to formally independent dedicated actors, named airport authorities. These are assigned the task of developing technical industry skills and thus, of providing a chance to improve the return on investment from airport operations by means of a long-term managerial approach. In this case, central political control should be limited to a macro-economic supervising activity consisting of the appointment of airports' top managers and, hopefully, to the sanction of illegal and anti-competitive practices by some actors. Airport authorities may be eventually privatised through direct transactions or stock flotation;
- mixed public/private control. In this case, private operators are actively involved in the management or in a partial ownership of airports. An excellent example is in the US, where airlines are frequently owners or exclusive concessionaires of terminals;
- private ownership programs. Exclusive private ownership has been blocked for a long time by the desire of public policies to maintain tight control of airport infrastructures. There are, however a few exceptions, such as the case of regional airports, like London City Airport. Figures show that until recently only 2% of the world's airports were owned by private operators. Trends toward privatisation, as for BAA Group or Wien Airport, are now, however, contributing to the increase in the number of players that can be included in the 'private ownership 'category. Tables 1.1 and 1.2 describe the main privatisation patterns that have occurred over the last number of years.

---

[3] The Authority usually refers to the Ministry of Transportation or to the Ministry of Defence.

Table 1.1 Airport privatisation through share flotation

Airport	Date	Type of sale
UK: BAA	1987	100% IPO
Austria: Vienna	1992	27% IPO
Denmark: Copenhagen	1994	25% IPO
	1996	24% secondary offering
Italy: Rome	1997	45,5% IPO
	2001	54,5% secondary offering
N. Zealand: Auckland	1998	51,6% IPO
Malaysia: Malaysian airports	1999	18% IPO
China: BCIA	2000	35% IPO and trade sale
Switzerland: Zurich	2000	22% IPO and 28% secondary offering

Source: Graham, 2001.

The Significant Fragmentation of Control

For decades airports have played the role of passive adopters of socio-political decisions by public governing bodies, regardless of their local, regional or national level. As a consequence, the entire airport industry has grown in a condition of significant fragmentation, as concentration would have limited the power of influence of local political forces.

On the one hand, national individualism made clear that each national player industry had to be able to stay independent in a strategic industry with no external influences. Moreover, airports are also local natural monopolies, putting them in a position to exert greater externalities on local communities compared with other sites.

These problems, that may be described in terms of 'competitive isolation', have underestimated the potential for co-evolution activities that could be achieved through the creation of constellations of players aimed at sharing costs and maximising current return on revenues.

Table 1.2 Airport privatisation through trade sales

Airport	Date	Share of apt. sold(%)	Buyer
UK: Liverpool	1990	76	British Aerospace
UK: Prestwick	1992	100	British Aerospace
UK: British Midlands	1993	100	National Express
UK: Southend	1994	100	RegionalApts. Ltd.
UK: Cardiff	1995	100	TBI
UK: Bournemouth	1995	100	National Express
UK: Belfast Int.al	1996	100	TBI
UK: Birmingham	1997	51	AerRianta/Natwest 40%, other private investors 11%
UK: Bristol	1997	51	Firstbus
UK: Liverpool	1997	76	Peel Holdings
Italy: Naples	1997	70	BAA
Australia: Brisbane, Melbourne, Perth	1997	100	various
Sweden: Skavsta Stockholm	1998	90	TBI
South Africa: ACSA	1998	20	ADRI South Africa Consortium (ADR has 69% share)
Germany: Hannover	1998	30	Frankfurt airports
N. Zealand: Wellington	1998	66	Infratil
Australia: 15 remaining major airports (excluding Sydney)	1998	100	various

Source: Graham, 2001.

Conduct like this, however, seems consistent with that performed by the main players in the air transport environment: airlines. In this case, public guidance in the form of 'flagship carriers' has for decades forced national operators to take irrational market decisions, like in the case of 'political driven' network planning, or forced personnel hiring during national employment crises.

Only recently, with smoothing of States' commandments as primary drivers of airline conducts, have we seen the development of co-evolutionary practices in the form of umbrella alliances, with the goal of both increasing market power and reducing the burden of deficits. This change in the rules of conduct for airlines has driven an increased level of turbulence in the airport business, too. Some signals of a turnaround are already present, whilst a number of projects are now being placed under scrutiny.

These practices seem to converge along three patterns of action:

- an equity-based participation in the ownership of the partner, this implying, however, the privatisation of the latter;
- the signing of a management contract agreement;
- non-equity based alliances, either strategic or operational, with a local or supranational scope.[4]

Industry-Specific Reasons for Low Competition in the Airport Industry

In some cases, we may take into consideration two additional industry-specific elements that may help to explain airport fragmentation. These are still acting as formidable obstacles against the adoption of proactive approaches by many airport operators.

The international regulatory framework of ASAs (Air Service Agreements) between two States partly explains this situation. In ASAs a limited number of two countries' airports are typically designated as gateways for outbound and incoming traffic movements. Most of the time these designated cities are the nation's capital and the main industrial or financial centres. In a situation like this, both airlines' productive decisions and customers' purchase choices are narrowed, with low margins of price negotiation being the next logical consequence.

The recent trend towards 'Open Skies'[5] policies has moved towards eliminating capacity caps whilst promoting the start-up of new services, when demand is sufficient to economically support these operations. These agreements, in fact, permit each carrier of the two signing States to fly to

---

[4] This will be explored in detail in Chapter 5.
[5] 'Open Skies' are liberal bilateral agreements promoted by the US Administration and signed with many European countries on an individual basis.

any destination without any regulatory obstacle, thus stimulating a proactive marketing approach by both airlines and airports as well.[6]

The same hub-and-spoke philosophy at the core of carriers' network management decisions, however, poses a technical threat to the chances of increasing the number of direct, non-stop links between airports.

This operational solution, in fact, requires an airline to concentrate most of its traffic movements on a hub-airport to maximise scale, scope, density and experience economies and reduce production costs of the service. Most of the airline's timetable will be flown not on a point-to-point basis, but on an indirect formula by means of offering the service through an intermediate hub stop. In the European context, the proliferation of hub systems within ASA constraints has frequently led flag carriers to search and then exploit an overlap between four types of airport roles: the technical hub concept (as benchmarked from the US experience); the political role of the city (and, as a consequence of that, of its airport as preferred rapid gateway for the State's capital); the function of the main city[7] as a nation's economic catalyser with related business traffic; and, finally, that of the airport as the airline's maintenance HQ.

Thus, we may say that carriers' capacity decisions and the intrusive control of States in the coordination of international traffic have been powerful elements in the marginalisation of non-core airports. This secondary market role has had for a long time, until the surge of deregulation practices, a negative impact on the economic value of non-hub airports, thus explaining their isolation and retrenchment into a modest local dimension, with no practical incentives to go proactively into the market.

The International Path of Evolution in the Airport Business

After a frenzy of privatisations and acquisitions in the late 1990s, the airport sector has remained relatively subdued over the last couple of years. The pick of new opportunities could arise from the proposed privatisation of Aeroports de Paris, which is expected to be launched by the French Government in 2005. Investors are also looking at Spain, hoping that the Government will soon take to the market the country's airport operator

---

[6] 'Open Skies' were promoted by the US in the early 1990s to increase the market presence of its national carriers along transatlantic routes.
[7] Which could also be other than the State's capital, as in the case of Zurich and Berne, for instance.

Aena. Amsterdam Schiphol is also short listed for privatisation, while in Asia plans to float Narita appear to be gaining momentum.

Although Europe represents some of the most significant financial opportunities, there could even be growth opportunities available in the US for airports willing to expand. Although US airport ownership has remained firmly in the hands of city and state, expectations are for opportunities to arise as airports seek to unlock the potential from the relatively undeveloped retail side of their business.

Both infrastructure groups and the major airport operators are likely to be ready to invest as new business opportunities arise in the years ahead. Airport investment opportunities, however, come with health warnings attached. A single decision from the regulator can radically affect the purchase value, like in the case of Fraport in the Philippines. Investors now tend to be wary of operators that are based around a single hub and are heavily reliant on a secondary flag carrier, like in the case of Unique, the operator of Zurich airport, and the collapse of Swissair.

Many financial decisions and investments tend to involve identifying the existence of a specific positioning for the airport and examining the level of interest of a carrier to base its operations there. An example of this is the development of the new Berlin airport, which is being strongly tied to the low-cost sector, given the relatively low proportion of business traffic at the German capital and the decision by EasyJet to establish a hub there.

Table 1.3 shows the economic performance of the world's 20 leading players in the airport business during 2003. Many of these players are high performers whilst at the same time public-owned and managed, showing that in this industry there is no definite link between profitability and private ownership.

Table 1.3 Top 20 airport groups by revenue ($m) – 2003

Apt. Group	Country	Main apt.	Group r.	Op.r.	Net.r.
BAA plc	UK	LHR/LGW/STN	2,953.9	903.9	835.5
Fraport	Germany	FRA	1,807.1	286.1	-114.8
Aena	Spain	MAD/BCN	1,594.3	197.8	42.7
Port Authority					
NY/NJ	USA	JFK/EWR/LGA	1,519.9	282.4	220.7
ADP	France	CDG/ORY	1,342.9	123.7	10.6
NAA	Japan	NRT	1,293.0	410.2	n.a.
KIA	Japan	KIX	872.3	n.a.	-128,3
Schiphol G.	Holland	AMS	750.6	240.2	133.7
H. Kong Apt.	China	HKG	694.6	109.2	64.4
Luftfart.t	Sweden	ARN	559.9	50.9	10.9
F. Munchen	Germany	MUC	544.9	50.2	6.2
City Chicago	USA	ORD/MDW	540.9	-4.0	n.a.
CAA Singapore					
	Singapore	SIN	527.1	169.1	103.3
Avinor	Norway	OSL	519.9	89.1	n.a.
ADR	Italy	FCO/CIA	507.5	107.5	8.0
SEA	Italy	MXP/LIN	490.6	51.0	14.3
LAW.Apt	USA	LAX	471.9	13.9	141.5
INFRAERO	Brazil	CPQ/GRU	470.1	176.7	58.7
SAA.	USA	SFO	465.2	55.5	62.1
Manchester Apt.					
	UK	MAN	460.2	88.9	3.3

Notes: For BAA, Marita, Kansai, Hong Kong, Singapore figures refers to March 2002-March 2003; for Fraport, Aena, NJ/NY, Aeroports de Paris, Schiphol, Luftfartswerket, Munchen, Chicago, Avinor, Aeroporti di Roma, SEA, INFRAERO figures refer to December 2001-December 2002; for Los Angeles and San Francisco figures refer to Jun 2001-Jun 2002; for Manchester figures refer to March 2001-March 2002.

Source: *Airline Business*, December 2003.

Chapter 2

The Air Transport Value Chain

The Air Transport Value Chain

In the current turbulent environment, the development and management of supplier-customer relationships is of primary strategic importance.

This observation seems much more significant when a so-called 'dilemma of complexity' takes place. This is linked to the dimensional and commercial fragmentation between a number of players. The most plausible reasons for this situation are related to competence-based barriers that require a deep specialisation in the output production and, thus, lead to limited technical interrelations between each value chain's sub-performances. Legal[1] or financial[2] constraints may impede a broader scope of diversification, too.

From a supply-side managerial perspective, this dispersion of market resources may be technically solved by one of the value chain's actors – known as the 'channel leader' – putting together single sub-outputs into unified value propositions. This condition is driven by the fact that, without active collaboration to jointly create value, the network as a whole will collapse, as customers will shift their purchasing intentions to other networked offers. Thus, in this case, one actor, usually the one that retains a market dominant position, activates a 'co-creation' process and every participant in the network collaborates according to the weight of its output.

From a demand-based view, this packaging role is much more significant where information asymmetries may impede direct negotiations between end customers and each individual provider, or when relevant tariff variance, due to price discrimination practices, takes place. Here it looks much more convenient for the customer to buy the assembled package rather than going unbundled.

---

[1] For example, dealing with specific stand-alone authorisation by States to produce a certain service.

[2] Linked to the high amount of cash resources needed to enter a specific business environment.

In the commercial aviation industry, the number of codified horizontal relations that exist between industry operators may be drawn within the *air transport value chain* framework.

Figure 2.1 illustrates the actors, positions, roles and main transactions between all industry players. A cursory glance proves that we face a deeply integrated meta-industry. The quality level of the final output – that is, a passenger/customer's travel experience – is related to the optimisation of all individual actions performed by a host of entities: airlines, airport enterprises, tour operators, travel agencies, and some specialised hard and soft providers. Finally, a crucial role is performed by public policies acting as 'metaregulators'[3] of all industry practices.

The Bundle of Actors Involved in the Air Transport Value-Chain

A quick look at the value chain as a whole must be however accompanied by a detailed analysis of each one of its players.

Airline Operators

In this category passenger carriers with different kinds of market positioning (luxury liners, flag carriers, national carriers, regional carriers, low-fare carriers, low-cost carriers, low-cost subsidiaries of network carriers, charter carriers) must be considered. Cargo operators and integrators[4] have to be included as well.

Luxury liners are those operators that offer a maximum level of quality in exchange for significantly high prices. An example is provided by Privat Air, a Swiss carrier that in cooperation with Lufthansa, flies daily from Düsseldorf to Newark in A319CJs and BBJs with only 48 seats. Prices are slightly higher than full business class fares and the niche target market is characterised by top managers of banks and multinationals.

Flag carriers are those industry players that still conserve significant monopoly rents in their served markets. We may refer to Asian countries, where tight regulations, in the form of single-designation ASAs, are still regulating city-pair traffics.

---

[3] In the previous chapter, the rather intrusive role of public policies in the management of aviation practices was already illustrated.

[4] Integrators are the direct heirs of what used to be referred to as "express couriers".

Figure 2.1 The air transport value chain: a static view

'METARULES' FIXED BY GOVERNING BODIES

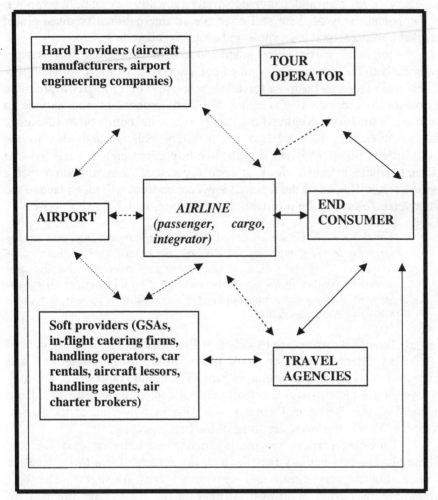

Note:

————	B2C (Business to Consumer) transactions;
- - - - - - -	B2B (Business to Business) transactions;
....	B2T (Business to Trade) transactions.

National carriers are the direct heirs of flag carriers in deregulated environments, in which they have been forced to reengineer their value proposition to compete with new start-up providers. US and European carriers, like British Airways, Alitalia, Air France and so on, belong in this category. Both flag and national carriers typically operate 'hub&spoke' systems and many of them still conserve an international or quasi-global market coverage, or at least show ambitions to adhere to it.

Regional carriers are small-to-medium[5] operators that usually provide both hub-feeder and point-to-point services for local communities. Their main target is business travellers who are willing to pay a premium price for the service in exchange for high frequencies and service to primary destinations. Regional carriers exploit some competitive advantage in operational costs, thanks to lower salary policies and also to the utilisation of highly efficient aircraft, like turboprops and regional jets that do not require a transit check at each flight leg.[6] It is rumoured that a widespread diffusion of the regional low-cost concept will take place in the next years, following the profitable experience of the UK carrier FlyBe.

> *For this reason, US unions have blocked major carriers from outsourcing services to regionals by means of so-called 'scope clauses'. A consequence of these clauses was stability of pilot salaries, but also increased rigidity in the economic choices of major carriers. The post-September 11 scenario has seen most of this rigidity disappear, at least in the North-American context.*

Low-fare carriers are usually non-flag operators which commenced operations after deregulation took place in the North American and European contexts. These operators provide a traditional service, but they charge on average 30-40% less than national competitors. British Midland in the UK, Air Berlin in Germany, Air One in Italy and, at its out-set, America West in the USA, are some of the best examples.

Low-cost carriers are placing major emphasis on cost savings. These players cut ancillary benefits and, in exchange for a lower level of service, launch very cheap and aggressive tariff packages.[7] The best example comes from Southwest Airlines in the USA, later imitated by Ryanair, its clone in Europe, and Virgin Blue in Australia.

---

[5] For instance, Comair, a fully-owned regional subsidiary of Delta Air Lines, has an all jet fleet of around 150 aircraft, not too far from Alitalia's fleet figures!

[6] These elements are frequently able to effectively counteract a theoretical higher cost-per-seat, due to the fewer number of seats that are boarded on regional aircraft.

[7] This concept is discussed in more detail in Chapter 4.

One of the most dynamic markets for low-cost carriers is Asia, where many start-ups have just taken off and more new entries have been announced (Ionides and O'Connell, 2004). Table 2.1 indicates current and future LC operators in the Far East.

Table 2.1 Selected Asia-Pacific low-cost carriers

Carrier	Base	Start date	Fleet
AirAsia	Kuala Lumpur	Jan 2002	737-300
Air Deccan	Bangalore	Aug 2003	ATR42, adding A320s
Air Do	Sapporo	Dec 1998	767-300ER
Cebu Pacific	Manila	Mar 1996	757-200, DC9
Freedom Air	Auckland	Dec 1995	737-300
Jetstar	Melbourne	May 2004	717, A320
Lion Airlines	Jakarta	June 2000	MD82-83
Nok Air	Bangkok	Jun 2004	737-400
One-Two-Go	Bangkok	Dec 2003	757-200
Pacific Blue	Christchurch	Jan 2004	737-800
Singapore AirAsia	Singapore	Tba	737-300
Skynet Asia	Miyazaki	Aug 2002	737-400
Skymark Airlines	Tokyo	Sept 1998	767-300ER
Thai AirAsia	Bangkok	Feb 2004	737-300
Tiger Airways	Singapore	Late 2004	Tba
Valuair	Singapore	Tba	A320
Virgin Blue	Brisbane	Aug 2000	737-700/800

Source: *Airline Business*, April 2004.

According to airline folklore, low-cost carriers have all based themselves on a single business model. Today, however, we may look at different market positioning even within the low-cost (LC) cluster. These are what we call 'hybrid LC operators'.

The latter differentiate their offer either by extending their range of in-flight services or focusing on different segments than the traditional ethnic-VFR[8] and tourist/student ones. On the one hand, JetBlue in the USA

---

[8] This is the acronym for Visiting Friends and Relatives.

provides in-flight entertainment, departure from some core airports (like New York's JFK), leather seats on board and so on. On the other hand, Easyjet in Europe targets business travellers by offering companies frequent services from major airports, like London Gatwick, Paris Orly and Milan Linate, at reasonable, but not necessarily the lowest, prices.

A subcategory of low-cost carriers is represented by flag and national carriers' low-cost subsidiaries. The choice to develop this 'airline-within-an-airline' concept has not produced consistent results. In the USA, United, Continental, Delta and US Airways have all closed their low-cost arms that had been created in the mid 1990s. However, United and Delta are now reviving two low-cost market experiments, named Ted and Song. Even in Europe this tendency looks controversial, with SAS planning to close its Snowflake subsidiary if losses continue. Table 2.2 illustrates the current 'airline-within-an-airline' international offer.

Table 2.2 Main international 'airlines-within-airlines'

Parent carrier	Low-cost brand
UAL	Ted
Delta Air Lines	Song
Lufthansa	Germanwings (through Eurowings)
Qantas	Australian Airlines
Qantas	Jetstar
Singapore Airlines	Tiger Airways
BMI	BMI Baby

Charter airlines have tour operators as their direct customer and often as their main shareholder,[9] in what is typically a B2B relationship. Charters' capacity is located along seaside and sunshine destinations, where demand for package holidays is highest, although there does tend to be significant variance according to the time of the year.[10]

Whilst in the US the charter cluster accounts for no more than 5%[11] of the total market, in Europe its presence is much more significant, with

---

[9] This happens in Europe, where Germany's TUI, the largest tour operator in the world, owns a package of national charter operators.

[10] In Europe, for instance, peak periods are July and August, Christmas and Easter. In the US, these peaks are slightly more smoothed, which helps explain the lower diffusion of the charter concept in the local airline industry.

[11] One of the main actors in the US is the Indianapolis-based carrier ATA.

around 30% of the industry's aggregate capacity. Nowadays, however, charter carriers are under intense attack by low-cost carriers. This has already led some of the main charter airlines to spin-off a low-cost subsidiary, like in the case of Germany's Hapag Lloyd with Hapag Lloyd Express and UK's My Travel with MyTravel Lite.

The difference between cargo carriers and integrators, finally, is an important one. Cargo carriers usually interact with freight forwarders and may be either arms of national/flag carriers (as in the case of Lufthansa Cargo and Korean Air Cargo) or dedicated, independent operators, like Cargolux in Europe and Atlas Air in the USA.

Integrators, on the other hand, are a logical evolution of express couriers: they integrate a multimodal package of solutions, usually road and air services, to pick up and deliver goods and documents to a final customer. This cluster is global and highly concentrated, with four players competing on a worldwide scale: DHL International, FedEx, UPS and TNT, with some minor providers, like Airborne Express, acting in some regional areas only.

These two sub-clusters of the cargo industry have been strictly separated for decades. Today there is a growing cannibalisation effect by integrators on cargo carriers' business, as even some forwarders are starting to ship via integrators to benefit from superior speed in the delivery process. Moreover, the cargo carriers have started to accept even heavy, bulky loads, where in the past their core activity was located in the handling of documents and small parcels. Some forms of alliances are now under way between cargo airlines and integrators.

> *Lufthansa Cargo and DHL are planning a strategic network alliance that will significantly boost DHL's ambitions in the global express parcel market while positioning the Lufthansa freight affiliate for an expected rebound in world air cargo traffic growth. The agreement runs through 2009, but both partners see the pact extending well beyond this timeframe. Lufthansa's partnership with DHL could be later expanded also to SAS, Singapore Airlines and Japan Airlines, its partners in the WOW cargo alliance.*

Airport Enterprises

The transition from airport platform, acting as a mere passive actor in the market, to airport enterprise, sees the latter becoming a manager of the various technical sub-activities[12] hosted within its boundaries. In this case,

---

[12] In this package of actors airlines are not considered.

the goal of airport management becomes profit maximisation from whatever source of business derived from a broader concept of 'flight experience', whether it be strictly related to aircraft services, or to more diversified value objectives.

Table 2.3 presents the two main strategic business units (SBUs) managed by an airport enterprise, known as the 'aviation-related' and 'non-aviation related' businesses. A market-oriented airport enterprise would consider as separate, even if highly correlated, the management of these businesses, with the goal of maximising overall returns on investment through competence-driven specialisation.

Table 2.3 The two main SBUs of the airport enterprise

Aviation-related activities	Non aviation-related activities
Landing fees	Rents from additional spaces to: airlines, General Sales Agents, catering firms, forwarders, cargo operators, tour operators, travel agents;
Air Traffic Control (ATC) fees	Rents and commissions from various commercial ventures (boutiques, duty free shops, banks, parking sites, etc.);
Passenger and cargo boarding fees	Direct sales arising from shops owned or managed directly by the airport authority;
Handling fees	Other complementary activities.

Whilst relationships between airlines and airports over charges are destined to get worse before they get better, with negative implications on the economic soundness of the aviation-related business, the prospects for non aviation activities seem to be improving, although at different rates from one airport to another.

Hard Providers

Aircraft and airframe manufacturers are included in this category as well as airport engineering companies responsible for the development or renovation of infrastructures.

In both cases, the final outcome, like the introduction of a new aircraft or the opening of a Greenfield terminal, always comes after a close partnership between: airlines and aircraft manufacturers; airlines and airports; airports and aircraft manufacturers; and airports and engineering companies. This kind of interface should take place from the very early concept phases and become stronger as the product's introduction approaches.

> *The challenge of the introduction of the new Airbus A380 involves encouraging selected airports to invest significant resources in upgrading their taxiways and parking spaces on the apron. Airbus and the other operators involved have established a close link since the first phases of the new Super-Jumbo's concept testing on the market.*

Usually, airport enterprises identify engineering companies as their primary counterparts, typically in the timing and implementation of their own master plans.

Soft Providers for the Aviation Business

In this broad category a diversified number of operators, each one with different roles, tasks and dimensions, may exist. The most important ones are:

- *General Sales Agents (GSAs)*, acting as sales representatives on a specific territory for airlines, hotel chains and car rentals. Nowadays there are a growing number of specialised domestic actors in this group. In the past, however, this role had been frequently played by airlines on a reciprocal basis. In this case, a carrier could identify a local operator – usually the national airline – as a counterpart on which to piggyback,[13] the former offering a similar sales support in its own mother territory.

---

[13] Piggyback is a term from the international marketing vocabulary. Technically, it means to exploit the existing sales network of an operator to distribute its own product or service.

For instance, Alitalia has acted for years as GSA for Air Algerie in Italy, whilst Air Algerie has done the same for Alitalia in its own market.

The use of GSA's leverage seems useful in the initial phases of a foreign entry strategy, when low volumes would not justify a direct sales force and, thus, a significant fixed cost base would not be tolerated. A GSA service is paid by commission on the basis of the actual amount of ticket transactions.

- *Airline catering operators* are responsible for providing supplies of food and beverage on board the aircraft prior to passengers' boarding. This industry is highly concentrated, with LSG (part of the Lufthansa Group) and Gate Gourmet (formerly a Swissair arm) counting for more than 40% of worldwide market shares. In a global context, however, there is still room for specialised niche operators, like Abela,[14] and for in-house departments of airlines, like in the case of many Asian carriers, that are frequently active only in the parent company's main hub. Table 2.4 provides figures concerning major in-flight catering suppliers for the airline industry.

- *Car rentals*, their strategic role in the air transport value chain being characterised by a growing number of multimodal bundled 'car+airline' solutions, a direct heir of the 'fly and drive' idea that dates back to the 1960s. In fact, in the absence of other accessibility solutions, cars represent the first method for feedering and defeedering airport platforms.

  One example comes from the UK, where low-cost operator EasyJet has created its own car rental company, named Easycar. Customers may book and purchase car rental services directly on the carrier's website with significant price promotions.

- *Aircraft lessors*, their task consisting in the activities of dry, financial and operating leases or leaseback[15] of aircraft to airlines. The use of a lessor may be justified for an airline as a way to compress aircraft delivery times. Lessors in fact place their own

---

[14] Abela is a specialised operator providing food for Moslems and Arab carriers.
[15] Many lessors offer more specific financial services, including spare parts, like engines.

orders at aircraft manufacturers that may be used for an airline customer.

> *GE.CAS, the acronym for General Electric Capital Aviation Services,[16] is the greatest operating lessor in the world. The company today owns more than 1.100 aircraft, which exceeds the number of owned fleet by any airline. The fact that GE.CAS is part of the General Electric empire helps to explain why the company has been established. In fact, starting a leasing unit proved to be useful for increasing the pace of production of turbofan, one of GE's core businesses, permitting the parent company to benefit from huge scale economies.*

Table 2.4 Major in-flight catering suppliers

Firm	Rev. 2001 $mil	Owner	HQ	Countries	Kitchens
LSG Sky Chefs	3,315	LH Group	Germany /USA	45	200
Gate Gourmet	1,957	TPG	Switzerland	31	140
Servair	408	Air France	France	18	30
Alpha Flight Services	388	Alpha Plc	UK	8	49
SATS	230	SQ Airlines	Singapore	7	9

Source: *Airline Business*, January 2003.

> *Today, around 30% of Airbus production is allocated to lessors. According to Airbus managers, this puts them in a 'comfort zone' when times get tougher. In the last downturn following September 11, only 11% of all delays, deferrals and cancellations came from leasing companies. Many industry analysts, however, consider*

---

[16] GECAS is very strong in the single-aisle leasing activities, whilst Los Angeles based ILFC is stronger in the wide body category. In absolute terms, however, GECAS has a greater number of owned aircraft in its portfolio.

this percentage of capacity allocated to lessors as being too high.
In other words, airlines wanting aircraft at short notice find
delivery slots already taken up by lessors and subsequently have
no choice but to opt for an operating lease.

- *Airport handlers*, their business being the production of terminal
  and apron services for the assistance of passenger and cargo
  aircraft, having airlines as counterparts. Table 2.5 takes a look at
  major players in the ground handling business, which shows the
  growing weight of third-party ground handlers which have no links
  with airport authorities or airlines.

Table 2.5 Major players in ground handling

Supplier	Rev. $m 2001	Owner	Stations	Countries	Main regions served
Globe Ground-Servisair	892	Penauille Polyservices	200	40	Worldwide
Swissport	668	Candover	160	29	Worldwide
Frankfurt AGS	524	Fraport	25	9	Europe, Africa
World Flight Services	344	Vinci	100	20	Europe, Americas, Asia
SATS	237	Singapore Airlines	6	5	Asia
Menzies	227	John Menzies plc	91	22	Europe, Americas, Asia
Avia Partner	187	Verougstraete Family (75%)	33	6	Europe

Source: *Airline Business*, January 2003.

- *Air charter brokers*, their task being to ease the contact between
  airlines and tour operators by brokering surplus airline capacity.

Tour Operators

Tour operators are one of the most well known 'package assemblers', their business consisting of putting together hotel stays, transportation, travel insurance and ground assistance.

On the one hand, airport enterprises interact with tour operators during negotiations concerning space rentals in the terminal complex needed to provide customer service activities.

On the other hand, airlines are a major supplier to tour operators, in the case of both scheduled and charter services.[17] Eventually, tour operators deal with travel agencies as their primary channel of distribution.

Travel agents

The role of the travel agent is a controversial one in air transport marketing (Shaw, 1999). This is due, on the one hand, from the fact that travel agents are the first trade partner for both airlines and tour operators, which pay agents a percentage of the value of the transaction, whilst also trading services of car rentals, cruises, railway operators and hotel chains.

On the other hand, their strategic role in the value chain comes from having a direct relationship with end customers. In fact, three quarters of air transport transactions are still being handled by travel agencies,[18] with other sales being processed by direct contact points, like Internet, call centres and airline passenger agencies.

Travel agents have traditionally benefited from information asymmetry between them and end customers. That asymmetry is rapidly disappearing in parallel with the massive diffusion of the Internet platform. As a consequence, travel agents may no longer assume a lack of transparency in prices and costs of air transport services to substain their own profit margins.

Thanks to the diffusion of the Internet, airlines are now able to bypass travel agents in all selling and relational links with end customers. This trend was initiated by low-cost carriers and now common among traditional operators, too. Huge distribution cost savings from direct sales permit airlines to effectively counteract the downward trend in yields that has been a constant occurrence for the last number of years.

---

[17] In some contexts, charter flights are not permitted by ASAs. In this case, such as on long-haul flights, tour operators buy and sell the seating capacity of scheduled airlines.

[18] This figure refers to the Italian market for 2003.

Not only however can the Internet be used as a B2C tool. Airlines have also developed some B2T (Business-To-Trade) platforms to maintain an open channel with major business travel agents. These companies, which usually operate on a multinational scope, typically manage all travel and travel-related needs of industrial and service companies. They are paid for by the customers through management fees or transaction fees and have abandoned the 'basic commission system' as a source of income, whilst putting great emphasis on acquisition of commission overrides.[19]

End Customer

It should now be clear that correctly identifying and targeting 'customers' rather than mere 'consumers' is a cornerstone of successful marketing in the airline industry (Shaw, 1999).

Customers represent the final subjects of all marketing actions, either single-sourced or packaged ones, by actors in the value chain. Their purchase decisions are influenced by a cognitive filter, represented by the image that the packaged offer, but frequently the single airline service due to its major visibility, has acquired over time in the market.

Channel Leader vs. Gate Guardian: the Two Primary Actors in the Air Transport Value Chain

In every value-chain system we may easily find actors with superior organisational capabilities which perform a systemic governance of processes and transactions.

Network's governance powers, of course, imply a chance not only to influence the quantity and quality of each sub performance to be bundled, but also a potential discrimination practice in the economic evaluation of single transactions.

This figure of *primus inter pares* will thus act to assemble each sub player's output and create an integrated value proposition. This position of political-economic-organisational command in value chain contexts is named *channel leadership*.

In the case of air transportation, airlines have been historically awarded the role of *channel leaders*, thanks to their superior dimensions in the scale and scope of operations and to significant socio-political and economic links, such as the ones mentioned in the previous chapter.

---

[19] The next paragraph will explain in more detail the differences between basic commissions and commission overrides.

Customers buy an airline ticket and the carrier becomes responsible for the guarantee of the overall service according to times and standards agreed at the moment of the sale. Thus, passengers consider airlines as their natural counterpart for all emerging issues, even when the problem can be related to an ancillary sub service. Moreover, as is the case with complex services production, customers could even not be aware of the existence of a number of different sub providers, exacerbating the negative impact of information asymmetries.

A second dominant role in value chains is played by those subjects that are managing a direct contact with end customers. These 'points of interaction' provide opportunities for collaboration and negotiations, explicit or implicit, between the customer and the company, as well as opportunities for those processes to break down (Pralahad and Ramaswamy, 2004). A closer interface may generate significant opportunistic advantages, as the value chain's gateway may bias customers' purchase decision by favouring its own economic interests instead. These actors are frequently referred to as *gate guardians* of the value chain.

Their marketing behaviour is usually passive, as their own service production will be activated by end customers; it is much more seldom that they show a proactive approach aimed at scouting new cluster targets, for instance on the basis of an increased level of endogenous competition.

In the air transportation context, the role of gate guardian is traditionally in the hands of travel agencies as the main channel of intermediation of the airline service.

Empirical evidence shows that travel agents frequently provide significant 'bias effect' on customers' choices. In fact, passengers are often persuaded to accept second-best options in terms of higher prices, lower quality of chosen carriers, longer total travel times and number of intermediate stops. This behavioural pattern is due to the standard rewarding scheme in use for an agent, which is based on a two-tier level of commissions. The traditional system calculated as a percentage of the value of tickets sold has been reinforced by the over use of 'commission overrides'. These are extra percentage points an airline will pay when the travel agent is able to consolidate a target level of its own ticket sales within a certain period of time. Another recent technique is the introduction of loyalty schemes for travel agents' employees that work in a similar way to the successful Frequent Flyer formula for passengers.

New Patterns of Conduct for Airport Enterprises: Skipping Peripheral Positions in the Value Chain

A systemic analysis of competitive conducts in the air transport value chain shows the relevant weakness and the secondary role that airport enterprises have played for a long time.

This can be explained firstly by the historical distance between airports and end customers: the latter having no direct link with the former and, thus, the main target of channel leaders and gate guardians. As a consequence of this passive role in B2C links, airports have for a long time been developing only process-based B2B transactions with airlines, tour operators, travel agents and other providers and delegating to these latter ones all the B2C marketing activity aimed to increase the airport's brand visibility. The effect of traffic increases was not, thus, directly linked to airports' commercial ingenuity, nor, at first, were the associated economic benefits gained by airports. Rather they went to the channel leader.

Deregulation processes in the channel leader's industry in the late 1970s would, however, dramatically change all the value chain's conducts. The same airport environment was eventually touched by these winds of change. In the early 1980s, best-in-class airports started to reinforce their negotiation powers with intermediate customers by means of more structured and proactive approaches in the form of market research studies as primary negotiating tools.

Moreover, airports started to think about ways to have a direct knowledge of end customers' priorities. This goal was achieved by a number of innovative – at least for the industry itself – direct marketing tools, with airports targeting potential passengers located in their own primary and secondary catchment areas for the first time. Local advertising, direct mailing and other publicity were used to improve the knowledge of services offered at airports for the target audience rather than a traditional presentation of airline network and frequency policies.

These combined tactics resulted in airports closing the historical gap that had divided them from end customers inside the air transport value chain. This momentum of change would be implemented within a broader change in managerial practices through new airport-specific marketing tools. The next few chapters will analyse in detail this new package of strategic and operational tools that may allow the airport enterprise to improve its relationship power in both B2B and B2C negotiations within the air transport value chain.

Chapter 3

The Aviation-Related SBU: The Airport Enterprise's Technical Core Business

The Traditional Value Proposition of Airport Enterprises

For many customers, airports represent a physical structure, some more or less spacious and comfortable than others, where they have to spend a certain amount of time to allow for the processing of technical requirements related to the 'flight experience'. Typical examples are check-in procedures for passengers and their baggage; passage through security inspections for accessing airside areas; and time spent waiting at boarding gates.

This picture of the airport environment in which the service encounter's technical aspects prevail, with inherently little difference between various players, seems to be a direct heritage of a *modus operandi* that has characterised industrial practices for decades.

Back in the early 1930s in North America, local political entities, like regions, counties and cities, started to realise the importance of having an airport in their own territory as it 'put them on the map' and improved their institutional visibility. In the same way, private entrepreneurs perceived airports as logistical platforms, and, thus, their fundamental role was in promoting and supporting commercial businesses thanks to a faster movement of incoming and outgoing passengers and goods (Valdani and Jarach, 1996).

These elements should provide clear evidence in understanding why this group of shareholders has for a long time considered airports as simple monomodal infrastructures, with a prominent focus on macro-political and economic targets rather than the achievement of a sound return on investment for the airport authority itself. This latter goal was considered secondary, with yearly losses to be covered through subsidies from local political communities. Figure 3.1 illustrates the various categories of stakeholders that influence and drive airport behaviour.

Figure 3.1 The package of stakeholders

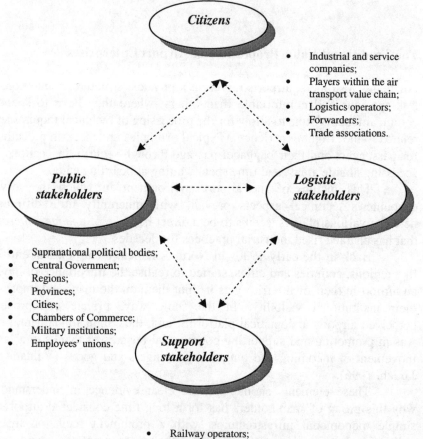

- Citizens living close to airport boundaries;
- Citizens living in the airport's catchment area;
- Citizens' associations.

Citizens

- Industrial and service companies;
- Players within the air transport value chain;
- Logistics operators;
- Forwarders;
- Trade associations.

Public stakeholders

Logistic stakeholders

- Supranational political bodies;
- Central Government;
- Regions;
- Provinces;
- Cities;
- Chambers of Commerce;
- Military institutions;
- Employees' unions.

Support stakeholders

- Railway operators;
- Motorway and freeway operators;
- Maritime operators;
- Other airport players (in the logic of alliance building and leveraging or within hub-and-spoke designs).

Source: Jarach, 2002.

At the end of the Second World War rigid global regulation of the industry led to the creation of high monopoly rents for airport players, thus reducing operating losses for airport players, to varying degrees, due to different levels of political interference.[1]

This would prove to be a formidable barrier to any sort of change in the years to come, resulting negatively on the spread of new managerial practices. One of the outcomes of this was visible in airport-airline relationships, where the former were clearly second-tier actors to the latter. In other words, airport managers were simply waiting for airlines to knock at their doors and, even then, the airports were providing a standard and undifferentiated offer to the carrier's bid, in the form of:

- availability of any slot in the time band of interest to the carrier;
- availability of apron and terminal spaces and/or maintenance facilities at the time needed by the airline;
- an estimation of landing and handling charges related to future airline landings;
- a possible scale of discounts on these fees on the basis of further movements (extra frequencies and routes).

One of the most significant weaknesses in airport management practices at the time was not having any effective estimates of the magnitude, density and economic importance of the airport's catchment area, other than by means of traditional and inadequate models of analysis.

This activity, which would have strengthened the strategic weight of an airport in B2B negotiations, was simply delegated to airlines' in-house skills and intelligence.[2] In other words, airlines were deciding their networks on the basis of their own information and simulation devices, whilst airports played no part in influencing the choice between two neighbouring sites.

During this time, airlines also acquired total control of the provider-customer relationship, whilst airports remained clueless about their passengers, except in terms of absolute numbers. This critical point would have seen some best-in-class airports develop, at the end of the century, their own dedicated loyalty programs.

From an organisational point of view, this reactive approach to market opportunities by airport managements helps to explain why marketing departments inside airport structures have for so long been either

---

[1] In the case of artificially high costs, due to politically imposed overstaffing for instance, monopolies simply permitted reduction of financial losses, but not their removal.

[2] It remains the case today that one of the main intelligence providers for the airline industry is represented by IATA, the airline industry association.

non-existent or hugely understaffed, despite the range of activities to be performed. In a best-case scenario, an existing marketing department was awarded scarce financial resources, because the need to perform studies or analyses as a value-added tool to be offered to intermediate customers was not recognised.

In the case where no marketing department existed, some of its tasks were undertaken by institutional relations or public relation bodies or directly performed by the top management as a way to enhance visibility in the media. Table 3.1 shows some quantitative evidence concerning the evolution of the marketing department in some UK airports. What is of particular interest is the significantly high passenger-per-staff member ratio that tends to decrease from the late 1990s'.

Table 3.1   Size of marketing departments at some British airports

Airport	Staff 1991	Staff 1997	Passengers-per-staff 1991	Passengers-per-staff 1997
Manchester	16	27	631,000	562,000
Birmingham	10	24	325,000	227,000
Newcastle	4	6	382,000	428,000
East Midlands	7	9	164,000	202,000
Bristol	7	6	392,000	248,000
Cardiff	2	6	257,000	185,000
Bournemouth	1	4	250,000	41,000
Norwich	1	5	215,000	54,000
Humberside	1	4	163,000	70,000

Source: Graham, 2001.

Note: we cannot provide corresponding data on passenger-per-staff indicators in other European airports. However, one should keep in mind the fact that the British market is at the forefront in Europe in terms of market proactiveness. Thus, we may suppose that figures from other contexts could be worse.

Summing up, until the beginning of the 1980s, the outlook in the airport business was characterised by a static approach by airports. This condition had the consequence of very rarely fostering any attempts to circumvent conventions and orthodoxies in this industry, with no incentive to adopt proactive strategies to increase both market share and power within the value chain. Entering the last decade of the century, however, things began to change drastically for industry players.

A Change in the 'Rules of the Game'

In the last two decades there has been a dramatic change in the codes of conduct for commercial aviation, with the transition from a public and protectionist view to a new private and hypercompetitive regime. This radical shift has made past market industry approaches obsolete.

This shakeout started at the end of the 1970s in the US, when airline deregulation was introduced. In the European market, on a similar basis, a three-step airline liberalisation process awarded carriers the flexibility to operate along every route of economic interest and connect any city pair within the Union's boundaries. This path of industry deregulation impacted on all airline practices, eventually reaching airports.

On the one hand, carriers were quick to reengineer their network designs by abandoning unprofitable routes and concentrating on core ones, with a parallel strategic scouting activity on emerging city pair connections. On the other hand, airports started to compete and attract carriers while striving to retain current ones. New airport facilities were being built on a greenfield basis or through the conversion of former military airports. This market turnaround was achieved by developing enlarged value proposition packages, where economic elements, in the form of supports for start-up operations or discounts on handling charges, started to become more and more prominent. This drove airports to develop a new managerial methodological approach to cope with their aviation-related business: we may say that airport marketing was born in this condition.

> *A three-way struggle is emerging in the battle for market share in the market for domestic and international travel to and from Russia's capital, Moscow. Domodedovo is continuing its ambitious expansion plans that aim to divert traffic from Sheremetyevo, where most of the international airlines operate. The site at Vnukovo, which is the smallest of the three airports and handles predominantly domestic traffic, could also be expected to play a greater role. In 2000, Sharemetyevo had a 64% share of passengers, falling to 48% in 2003. Vnukovo also saw a fall, from 20% to 12%. Domodedovo's share, instead, climbed to 40% in 2003 from 16% in 2000, on the back of an aggressive development program, and success in wooing new carriers to the airport. For instance, British Airways was one of the prestige carriers that switched to Domodedovo from Sheremetyevo.*

For future performance improvements, the Russian government is looking to select a private management company as a strategic partner for the state-owned Sheremetyevo airport. Table 3.2 shows the split of actual operations between Moscow's three airports.

Table 3.2   Analysis of services at Moscow's Airports as of December 2002

Airport	Weekly flights	Share	To Russia	To other CIS States	To Western Europe	To Eastern Europe
Sheremetyevo	1,050	54.6%	36.5%	9.6%	33.6%	9.5%
Domodedovo	566	29.5%	66.5%	24.3%	6.2%	0.6%
Vnukovo	300	15.6%	69.4%	27.0%	1.4%	0.0%
TOTAL	1,923	99.6%	50.7%	16.6%	20.4%	5.4%

Source: OAG timetable.

Airports in the Middle East are racing to complete nearly $10 billion worth of expansion projects. Qatar has planned a $2-billion project at Doha International Airport which will enable it to handle 12 million annual passengers in 2008 and 15 million in 2015. Meanwhile, Dubai's $4,1-billion expansion will allow it to handle 40 million passengers by 2010 and 100 million by 2025. Abu Dhabi plans a $600-million expansion that includes a new terminal for 2005 which will increase capacity to 8 million passengers, while Bahrain's international airport is undergoing upgrades valued at $120-million.

The Rise of Airport Marketing for the Aviation-Related Business

In the early '90s, the new enriched value-based package of airport enterprises started to include:

- co-marketing and co-branding partnerships between airports and airline operators or other value chain players, like tour operators and travel agencies, with the goal of improving territorial coverage;
- road shows at carriers' headquarters to illustrate both technical facilities and market research studies on the airport's catchment area, the latter having become primary drivers to identify the scope for new flight services;

- presence at industry fairs, like Routes or Networks,[3] or events concerning the whole tourism industry, like the World Travel Market in London;
- definition of economic schemes for carriers, referred to as marketing support system plans (MSSP), with the aim to cut monetary incentives associated with the opening of new air connections;
- aggressive handling charges, no longer based on the 'cost per ton' system, but restructured by categories of aircraft with similar flight performances. In the old system, airport management would have offered large discounts, especially in the first phase of operations in accordance with the support system plan previously mentioned.

As a consequence of this approach, some carriers would have readjusted the structure of their networks, for instance, by introducing capacity on routes serving secondary, less congested and cheaper airport facilities: as is the case for many low-cost carriers.

> *We may refer to the historic behaviour and conduct of Buzz, Ryanair and Go. All these carriers have chosen to base their operations at London's Stansted airport, which is cheaper due to its more peripheral location compared with Heathrow and Gatwick, the latter also playing a hub role that is absent in the case of Stansted. All three airports are managed by the British Airport Authority Group (BAA plc.).*

Concerning these points, Figure 3.3 illustrates the main factors influencing the choice of airport by an airline operator. The hierarchy of significance of these factors may change depending on the type of carrier in question and can also be correlated to the market positioning of the airline itself.

> *Ryanair, when deciding on the location for its second and third European hubs, chose other off-city, secondary airports. These airports are sometimes an 80 min. drive from downtown, but are uncongested and thus permit the carrier to maintain its tight turnaround policy which is at the core of its business model. In this sense, the Irish carrier chose Hahn rather that Frankfurt Main (both, however, managed by Fraport) and Charleroi rather than Brussels' Zaventem.*

---

[3] Routes is the main European fair for the air transportation industry. It takes place on an annual basis and is always hosted in a different location. Network is the US equivalent of Routes.

Figure 3.2   Main elements involved in airport choice

- Width, density and potential market growth of the catchment area;
- Slot availability;
- Presence or absence of direct competitors;
- Network and operational consistency;
- Airport charges (landing and handling fees plus fuel prices);
- Minimum guaranteed turnaround times;
- Presence of economic and commercial incentives at start-up of operations;
- Width and availability of airport infrastructural facilities;
- Availability of a range of intermodal solutions for accessing and leaving the airport;
- Absence of environmental restrictions (fundamental in the case of overnight cargo services);
- Availability of maintenance centres at the airport;
- 24 hrs. non stop opening times (again, critical in the case of cargo);
- Presence of upgrade projects for terminal expansion;
- Low historical rate of accidents on apron caused by handling operations.

The large urban hinterland area of London today hosts seven airports, each one struggling to attract extra passengers or cargo on the basis of a specific positioning. Heathrow competes as a global primary hub, Gatwick is more of a leisure-oriented, charter airport; whilst Stansted is home to the main low-cost operators. London City Airport provides business access to the financial district of the British capital, whilst Luton is transforming itself to host a growing range of point-to-point, LCC traffic. Biggin-Hill is one of the UK's best-known airports, having been one of the main RAF stations during the Battle of Britain and home to the annual air show. Over the last 40 years it has also undergone a gradual metamorphosis into the busy commercial airport it is today. Biggin Hill, which is only 12 miles from the centre of London can cope with aircraft up to the size of a B737 and has a number of private charter operators based there. Manston Airport offers some maintenance and technical facilities and seems focused on cargo traffic, with MAS (Malaysian Airlines Cargo) as one of its core customers.

A similar scenario exists in the Milan area. Linate airport, close to downtown Milan, hosts at present strong point-to-point, business traffic, whilst the more distant Malpensa strives to act as a primary hub for Southern Europe. Orio al Serio airport, actually closer to Bergamo than to Milan, hosts low-cost carriers and a minor share of the catchment area's charter traffic.

Airport's Market Positioning

This kind of strategic decision seems today to be at the core of the commercial policy of the airport-enterprise. On the basis of the distinctive features of each individual airport, a consistent positioning strategy is a preliminary step in the design of all operational airport marketing tools, such as:

- *definition of the level and content of the value proposition*, or, in other words, of the offer that will be presented to the potential audience by the value chain's intermediate customers and end consumers;
- *identification of the price level*, or of the price band, that an airport-enterprise will charge its intermediate customers for the bundle of services produced;
- *implementation of the communication campaign* that an airport-enterprise will launch to capture the attention of operators or political stakeholders;
- *Level of distribution of the value proposition*, this element referring to the coverage and penetration levels that an airport will choose to reach in its primary catchment area and, eventually, attacking the competitive field controlled by other industry players (the so called secondary catchment area).

To achieve the correct market positioning, an airport-enterprise will need to implement an exploratory market research study, aimed at understanding both the quantity/quality of current traffic values and the potential purchase intentions of its catchment area. This path seems fundamental to generate a consistent value system which matches the target's needs. Each geo-commercial area will show different trends due to a stronger business-industrial or leisure-tourist element; for example, the different quantity and quality of traffic that influence movements in Verona, Italy (mainly an industrial area) or Palma de Majorca, Spain (a typical sunshine destination) are clearly visible. Nethertheless, airports may decide to differentiate their offer system and abandon local demand connotations. This process, however, seems much more risky and is likely only to be activated in the case of dramatic market growth by a new offer cluster, like LCCs.

On the basis of this analysis, an airport will have to choose between *three different positioning strategies*.

The first one refers to a competitive market positioning, in which an airport is in open and direct competition with other airports, on the basis of parameters like geographical proximity or the type of operations hosted, e.g. point-to-point vs. hubbing activities.

The second strategy refers to a niche market positioning, that aims at avoiding an open confrontation with other players. This option will be adopted when financial and management resources are lacking. It will be successfully implemented when technical or infrastructural weaknesses can *ex ante* impede airport activities on a competitive arena, as in the case of London City or Düsseldorf City airports.

A third and final option may see airports gaining a specific market positioning as a result of their association with an airport alliance. This positioning strategy will have to be a complementary and synergic one to those of to the ones of other allied partners.

Referring to the possible types of positioning that an airport may adopt within a chosen positioning strategy, we may count five different alternatives.

Primary Hub

Here the airport enterprise aims to operate as a hub focusing on facilitating passengers and goods travelling on a transnational level. This goal will be best achieved by first attracting one or, possibly, a couple of airlines that will develop their main base of operations[4] at the airport.

In this sense, it's critical to note that the role, strategies and performance of the hub carrier are key in terms of the growth potential and long-term economic viability of the primary hub airport. Network rationalisation, when accompanied by severe flight cuts, will drastically impact on the hub's attractiveness to the market, whilst a steady increase in served destinations will improve its market visibility, especially for connecting traffic.

---

[4] The so called hub carriers or hub makers.

Munich airport, although located in a smaller and less wealthy area than Milan Malpensa airport, has seen steady passenger growth for the last few years thanks to the significant capacity growth of Lufthansa, the hub carrier. In contrast, Alitalia's network cuts, especially after September 11, have drastically reduced the chances for Malpensa to become a primary player in the Southern European region.

Primary hubs have historically been developed at major political and business locations. In these locations, the hub carrier will be able to count on a significant base of O&D (Origin & Destination) traffic. The airline will create opportunities for growth in connecting and transit traffic due to its links with spoke destinations.

Some airports, however, have reinforced their position as primary hubs, not only through online traffic by the hub carrier, but also due to huge interlining traffic agreements between non-partner carriers.[5]

This is the case of London Heathrow, for instance, which is historically considered by US travellers as the main European gateway, thanks to the unmatched level of frequencies along US-UK city-pair destinations. Many American travellers choose to fly with a US carrier[6] and then stop in London and board another operator to reach their final destination.

The primary hub formula targets both business and leisure, thanks to the large amount of system capacity offered to and from the airport by the hub carrier. Nevertheless, some airports have stretched their role of primary hubs by including cargo traffic. For instance, Amsterdam, London Heathrow, Frankfurt and Paris CDG are the main players in the cargo business even if their primary focus remains passenger traffic. The development of cargo as a complementary activity is possible thanks to the availability of belly-offer on passenger and combi flights, as well as dedicated cargo-only flights to some of the main destinations.

Secondary Hub

An airport enterprise with a secondary-hub objective acts within a smaller geographical and commercial horizon than that of primary hubs. In fact,

---

[5] Non-partner carriers means that airlines are not members of the same umbrella-alliance, like Star or Sky team. They simply cooperate on an operational basis by interlining their fares and flights.

[6] For example, diplomats and Pentagon contractors, who are forced by law to fly with a US carrier.

this kind of airport aims to manage, almost exclusively, connecting traffic
on a regional basis.

The location of secondary hubs is similar to that of primary hubs,
that is in regional business or leisure centres with strong O&D inbound and
outbound traffic: as is the case of Barcelona, Clermont Ferrant, Basel,
Seattle, St. Louis,[7] Mumbai and Nairobi. Frequently secondary hubs
emerge at airports where a previous primary hub project has collapsed, due
to insignificant local demand or to the hub carrier's bankruptcy, as in the
case of Zurich and Brussels.

The commercial success of secondary hubs can be related to lower
congestion levels that permit smoother transfer times, as is the case of
Clermont Ferrant in France. This tiny airport, established to serve
Michelin's[8] travel needs, has operated for several years as a secondary hub,
competing with Paris CDG to attract business connecting traffic. This was
possible thanks to the lower number of aircraft operations, with a positive
impact on the efficiency of technical hubbing procedures, and to a strong
partner carrier, Regional Airlines. When this airline was bought by Air
France, the French national carrier decided to limit hubbing operations in
Clermont Ferrant to reduce cannibalisation with Paris CDG.

Regional Airport

These airports usually manage 10-15 million passengers per year. They do
not host any hub carrier as they traditionally play the role of spokes within
major airlines' networks. Regional airports promote a significant offer of
regional carriers, the latter acting independently or through a bundle of
different partnerships[9] with network airlines. Regional airports tend to
focus on point-to-point traffic, with very little connecting traffic.

The commercial success of a regional airport relies mainly on the
chance to exploit a favourable geographic location and proximity to a city's
downtown area. Some best-in-class examples from this category are Turin
and Venice in Italy, Valencia in Spain, Düsseldorf and Stuttgart in
Germany, Nice in France, and La Guardia in New York.

A subcategory of the regional airport model is provided by city
airports. These operate inside city boundaries and, for this reason, are
usually subject to some operational limitations in take-off and landing

---

[7] After TWA's collapse.
[8] Michelin's world HQs are located at Clermont Ferrant.
[9] These ones could be in the form of code-sharing, soft or hard-block space
agreements or franchising.

procedures or in the type of aircraft permitted. City airports serve exclusively business targets that are willing to pay a premium for a closer-to-city departure point, faster handling services and a huge number of point-to-point services to the main regional financial centres.

Traditionally, city airports are secondary airports, close to city boundaries or within them, that have a lower number of movements and passengers than other airports in the same area for the following reasons:

- *current constraints in the infrastructural package, like short runways, or tiny terminal and apron spaces.*
- *technical limitations, due to obstacles that may impact on take-off and landing procedures;*
- *operational and environmental regulations that are aimed at preserving the quality of life of neighbouring residents.*

Due to these constraints and limitations, these airports have played for decades a marginal role in the market. In the last decade, however, some of these players have been able to turn these elements of competitive disadvantage into critical factors of success, thanks also to the growing congestion of the primary sites. First of all, city airports have identified regional carriers as their main partners. These carriers usually manage small aircraft, turboprop or jet ones, and are primarily interested in providing point-to-point connections between regional and main business locations. Their target customers are typically business travellers, willing to pay higher tariffs in exchange for non-stop air links rather than having to stopover at hubs.

The strategic profile of today's best-in-class city airports, however, sees a significant differentiation of the whole value proposition to the customers. For instance, business travellers usually like to shorten their staying times at terminal buildings to maximise their work time. At London City Airport, thus, passengers may check-in up to 10 minutes before departure. Again, another perceived KPI (Key Performance Index) by the customers, like baggage delivery times to incoming passengers, will be much shorter than at hubs, thanks to efficient cooperation between the airport authority and ground handling operators.

City airports do not provide customers with a different package of routes and air services than other airports they have, instead, reengineered their value proposition around KPIs to stay in touch with the expressed needs of their target audience. Of course, this should be a fundamental rule of airport management.

A second subcategory of regional airports is represented by charter airports, which host the seasonal traffic of charter carriers. Here the target cluster becomes a purely leisure one and the range and bundle of services offered will be reduced to stay in touch with the strict economic requests by airline operators. Many airports included in this category are now evolving themselves into the paradigm of low-cost airports.[10]

> *A typical example of a charter airport is Crete's Heraklion airport in Greece. This airport has a complete reversal of operations from winter to summer. In the latter case, take-off and landings are separated by just a couple of minutes! This creates a lot of pressure on the terminal and apron infrastructures, and new buildings are now being constructed to cope with peak demand. However, there is a problem concerning the inefficient utilisation of infrastructures during winter seasons, which increases the annual management costs of the airport.*

All-Cargo Airport

The main distinctive feature of this cluster of airports is that they are fully dedicated to the cargo business, thanks to a package of state-of-the-art intermodal solutions (rail, road and sometimes, water).

By exploiting a favourable location, which is usually far from cities to avoid environmental limitations,[11] this kind of infrastructure may be able to operate on a 24 hour basis.

> *There are still a few examples of all-cargo airports in the international arena. One of them is Euro port Vatry, located 150 km. from Paris, that entered into service in 2000. In Asia, Subic Bay in the Philippines, a former USAF base, now acts as an all-cargo airport for FedEx.*

More Positioning Criteria

The above framework which categorises airport positioning strategies into five main areas is, of course, a simplification of the actual situation which exists in the airport industry.

In fact, there exists much higher variance, due to the combination of both endogenous and exogenous factors. Table 3.4 shows 19 different market positionings, that have been identified on a basis of worldwide empirical research.

---

[10] Chapter 4 will discuss the 'low-cost airport' concept.
[11] This reduces the environmental impact of airport operations and, thus, prevents the introduction of rules limiting aircraft take-offs and landings.

Table 3.3 Nineteen different airport positioning criteria

	Market positioning	Examples of airports located in the described category
1	Airports integrated into a city's marketing plan	Manchester
2	Airports integrated into a region's (or federal state's) marketing plan	Munich
3	Airports with growth potential, although limited by physical constraints	Brussels San Francisco Amsterdam
4	Airports integrated within a system and where the same hub carrier is dominant	Paris Orly and CDG London Heathrow and Gatwick
5	Airports integrated within a system by the will of a regulator	Milan Linate and Malpensa Tokyo Haneda and Narita, Washington Dulles and Reagan
6	Airports operating within the same catchment area, although with different value propositions	Chicago O'Hare and Midway Stockholm Arlanda and Bromma Milan Malpensa and Orio
7	Airports attracting overflow traffic	London Biggin Hill Paris Le Bourget Rome Ciampino
8	Airports with an alternative (low-cost) proposition	London Luton and Stansted Paris Beauvois Brussels Charleroi Milan Orio Frankfurt Hahn
9	Airports implementing cooperative policies with neighbouring residents and counties	Frankfurt, Amsterdam, Tokyo Narita
10	Airports with technical limitations (city airports)	London City Airport Florence

		Toronto City Courchevel Chambery Düsseldorf Express Aosta
11	Airports under reengineering, due to abandonment by the hub carrier	St.Louis, Raleigh-Durham London Gatwick Geneva
12	Airports designated as national or pan regional gateways (primary and secondary hubs)	Wien, Miami Toronto Johannesburg Dubai Los Angeles Bangkok New York JFK
13	Airports with a cargo focus (all-cargo airports)	Vatry Rotterdam (scheduled) Memphis Louisville Luik
14	Greenfield airports	Munich Oslo Seoul Athens
15	Upgraded airports, on the basis of previously existing infrastructures	London Heathrow Milan Malpensa Doha Dubai Bahrain Madrid Paris CDG
16	Airports with limitations in the range of air services offered, due to infrastructural constraints	New York La Guardia Tokyo Narita Washington Reagan
17	Airports acting as a country's sole gateway	Singapore Hong Kong Malta Larnaca/Nicosia
18	Airports undergoing conversion	

	from military to civil operations	Torrejon (Spain)
		El Toro (California)
		Grazzanise (Italy)
19	Dominant airports (not the sole country's gateway, but controlling most of the market)	Helsinki
		Copenhagen
		Tel Aviv
		Wien
		San Juan
		Dublin

A Clear View of its Role on the Market

Construction of terminal buildings and infrastructures alone doesn't automatically imply that the airport will be on the right track for success. In the absence of serious managerial efforts, some traffic volumes will probably be achieved by chance, but this volatile performance will not provide long-term economic viability for the airport enterprise.

Thus, as part of the feasibility study of the airport project, a full-scale strategic marketing analysis will be needed to quantify both the width and the density of the airport's catchment area. This is the area where most of the local traffic comes from and so will be where airport enterprises concentrate their marketing efforts.

The catchment area is a dynamic rather than static measure that has to be constantly reviewed and revised, as it may change not only depending on the destination being served (short-haul vs. medium or long-haul), but also on the type of SBU involved (aviation vs. non-aviation related activities). In the latter case, for instance, we will have different commercial catchment areas according to the various types of non-aviation businesses (commercial, conference, tourist, logistic, consulting).

The most basic approach to defining a catchment area is on the basis of drive time – typically one hour. Isochrones of longer times may represent secondary catchment areas (or 'areas of opportunity'). These areas will be subject to greater degrees of contestability as they may overlap with other airports. The airport's marketing efforts will concentrate on these areas only when the primary catchment area (also referred to as the 'comfort zone') is fully covered (Graham, 2001).

The size of the primary catchment area and the proportion of it's inhabitants who are likely to fly will depend on factors such as the quality of road networks, the economic, business and tourist activity within the area, the demographic characteristics of the residents and the competing services at other airports. In this sense, improvements in the road infrastructure or public transport can significantly alter the catchment size. Figure 3.3 sums up the main drivers of dimension and density for a primary catchment area.

An updated method of calculating catchment areas is based on the so-called 'geomarketing + O&D (Origin Destination)'. Through the analysis of BSP and MIDT[12] data, an analyst may identify zones that are actually part of an airport's 'zone of attraction' even if these areas are outside it's the airport's primary catchment area. Using this more refined method will give the catchment area a different shape from the one commonly drawn as circles, including external areas but also depriving from the airport's target zone nearby places, for instance, where ticket sales show a preference for another airport site.

Identification of Partners for Airport Development

The airport enterprise will have to search for one or more airline partners to jointly plan and develop new air services from the airport or improve existing ones for the target audience.

In this case, airports will contact carriers and present market research studies concerning the width and density of the catchment area, its economic potential and the package of incentives and supports that the airport will grant for the start-up of new connections.

The latter will be based on the so-called 'Marketing Support System Plan' (MSSP) formula. Airports will give carriers a certain amount of money (which will change from carrier to carrier) as a support for promotional initiatives in the media about the launch of the new route and to partially cover initial start-up costs, when load-factors are usually below break-even points. The issue of airports providing incentives, or even hard cash support, in order to win airline service is hardly new and has been a recurring theme over recent years. Since 1993, when Manchester Airport pioneered the concept of a support package to bring American Airlines to the Northern English city earlier than the carrier originally planned, regions and airports have created increasingly sophisticated and generous incentives to attract airlines (Pilling and Pinkham, 2003).

---

[12] BSP and MIDT are two common databases used in the airline industry. The former provides figures concerning sales from travel agents, whilst the latter is related with bookings made through the main Global Distribution Systems (GDS).

Figure 3.3   Key drivers impacting on the size of an airport's catchment area

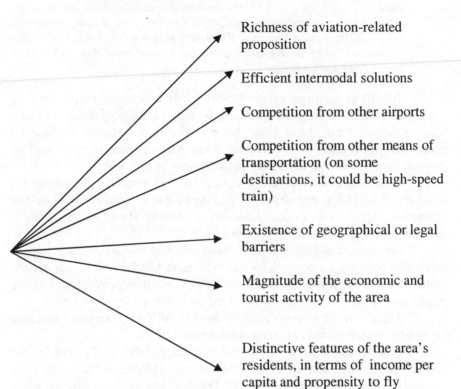

Richness of aviation-related proposition

Efficient intermodal solutions

Competition from other airports

Competition from other means of transportation (on some destinations, it could be high-speed train)

Existence of geographical or legal barriers

Magnitude of the economic and tourist activity of the area

Distinctive features of the area's residents, in terms of income per capita and propensity to fly

Nowadays, with a recovery in traffic levels looking more realistic, there is added incentive for communities, especially in small and midsize cities, to lure new carriers, often to replace services lost over the past two years of crisis (Pilling and Field, 2004). Airlines warn that routes have to be viable without support at some point, although any incentive that mitigates entry into the market is helpful. In any case, any monetary incentives, either marketing incentives or subsidies, should always be backed by a sound route analysis and communities should not throw all their money at the first airline that comes along.

Since November 2002, when Scotland first established its three-year £6.8 million Route Development Fund, 13 new routes to Scottish airports have been secured.

The potential scale of the cash on offer from communities was demonstrated by Portland's bid to win European air services. The state of

Oregon put in place an $11 million travel bank that helped tempt Lufthansa into launching a daily Frankfurt service in mid-2003. Under such an arrangement, a local community creates a bank account into which businesses and individuals pay to fly on the airline being supported. It is in effect a guarantee from the private sector to use the carrier. When flights are taken on the airline, the businesses draw down from their travel bank accounts.

A typical recipient of the MSSP formula is today represented by low-cost carriers. These operators look for this package of incentives as a way to sustain their cheap fares that would not be possible without an economic contribution by airport authorities. Airport enterprises are willing to grant these economic incentives for a number of reasons.

First, the impact of a low-cost carrier, in terms of the passenger numbers, is huge for any airport. This feature has a positive effect on the amount of passenger taxes raised and can, moreover, stimulate purchases at the various non-aviation corners at terminals.

Second, low-cost carriers have a positive economic impact especially on tourist areas, where the increasing number of tourists means higher occupation levels of hotels and villas, whist improving real estate prices, too. A typical example is provided by Southern Spain and Nice.

Third, a rapid increase in the airport's traffic may require a terminal expansion, which would create local job opportunities.

Fourth, low-cost carriers stimulate intermodality: Ryanair is the number one on-line broker of Hertz in Europe, whilst EasyJet has its own car rental company, named EasyCar. Overall, low-cost carriers promote demand for car rental services, although these volume increases may also mean a decrease in per-rental yields.

Moreover, the opening of 'flagship routes' from secondary airports at very low fares may have a significant political impact, especially in the case of public-owned and managed airports. In this case, the start-up of low-cost carrier routes may be a driver of growing support for local politicians.

In the US, Jet Blue does not look for incentives to start up new routes. It is much more interested in long-term airport costs and the need to make the route work in the long-term. On the contrary, Delta Air Lines routinely asks for revenue guarantees from communities that want a new service to be established, to cut start-up times that, for a regional jet service, are of two years.

After the recent Ryanair-Charleroi case, European airports are now allowed to develop joint marketing plans with carriers with a time period not exceeding five years. Moreover, handling discounts are forbidden if applied discriminatorily to a single carrier, whilst acceptable if it is part of a market policy by the airport to differentiate it from neighbouring airports and is open to all airlines. Of course, this price discrimination would have to be consistent with airport's profit aims.

> *Ryanair asked Polish Airports State Enterprise (PPL) for a passenger charge of €5 to cover all landing fees and services if it served Warsaw. Polish managers were forced to refuse, as the normal price the airport charges per departing passenger is €16 and the proposed sum would not cover airport's costs.*

One of the problems faced by an airport authority in the search for an airline partner, especially in the case of small, low-visibility sites, is the existence of 'cherry pickers'.

This type of actor will maximise its short-term benefits by negotiating a significant package of economic incentives from the airport. Instead of partly investing these sums in promotional campaigns, this carrier will simply consider MSSP as a subsidy and will practically act as a charter carrier. In other words, when the money is gone, the airline will immediately stop operations. In this case, the damage for the airport is huge, as long-term, sustainable traffic growth has not been generated. Politicians may be happy enough in attracting an airline, even if it turns out to be a 'cherry picker', due to the short-term perspective of the political mind-set.

> *Tallahassee, Florida and Wichita, Kansas, each spent heavily to attract low-cost Air Tran Airways, but the Orlando-based airline has scaled back flights and is uncertain if it will stay in Wichita when its two-year agreement there ends in May 2004.*

Of course, with carriers' proliferation in the post-deregulation environment, the number of 'cherry pickers' has increased, too. The ultimate goal of these players and of their owners is simply to exploit all opportunities that may arise, by imposing their power on weaker players, such as secondary or almost abandoned sites.

Airports, however, have to build their own partnership networks by involving other value chain operators. For instance, the power of attraction that charter carriers may produce on airports is directly correlated with their partnerships with tour operators, which may however decide to centralise their leisure operations on a specific airport. Again, the creation of a maintenance base by an independent player may be an opportunity to attract new carriers to the airport enterprise. The relationship between an airport and travel agents in its catchment area is crucial, as their power of influence on the final customer might shift traffic to other competitors. A partnership between the airport authority and an independent car rental outlet may build a *de facto* intermodal platform and, thus, provide a solution in the case of inefficient road and rail connections. Finally, an established relationship between the airport and a catering unit is an element of strength, as, otherwise, carriers would be forced to embark both incoming and outgoing food with operational weight limitations to be applied.

Chapter 4

New Marketing-Driven Paradigms for the Airport Enterprise's Aviation-Related Business

The First 'Quantum Leap' of the Airport Enterprise

Evidence from industry practice shows that best-in-class players are moving away from classical 'mono-modal' approaches, where airports struggle between each other and with other modes of transportation to increase the weight of their demand. In fact, these actors are developing new strategic models based on co-evolutionary designs with other transportation solutions. The path of cooperating with a competitor inside its own value proposition, either a direct one or another transport operator, seems effective, most definitely in those environments, like Europe, where airlines compete according to market conditions, whilst other providers, like train operators, are hugely subsidized by their State owners. Here airport enterprises abandon their 'splendid isolation' within a country's logistics package and provide the initial momentum for radical change, or a 'quantum leap', towards a *multimodal hub* approach. The customers' of multimodal hubs (either passengers or goods) are given the chance to seamlessly connect from air to ground, railway and sea ferry[1] within airport boundaries. This integrated and upgraded bundle on offer naturally improves the chances for airports to foster their market power, thanks to the combined use of airport infrastructure, high-speed trains[2] and motorways. Best practices, when dealing with European players, refer to Charles de Gaulle airport in Paris, Frankfurt airport in Frankfurt and Schiphol airport in Amsterdam. The adoption of an intermodal approach has given these sites not only the opportunity to expand their passenger-catchment areas, crossing regional or national borders, but also to increase the weight and

---

[1] As in the Scandinavian context.
[2] On the other hand, the use of trains as a commuting medium to connect the airport with its own city seems consistent with the classical mono-modal approach.

number of business-to-business transactions. FedEx, for instance, chose Paris CDG as its European hub thanks to its superior intermodal infrastructures, a *must* for logistics and cargo operations.

> *Paris Charles de Gaulle (CDG) is considered one of the best intermodal airports in the world. Thanks to a seamless interconnection with TGV (French high-speed train) directly inside the terminal buildings, CDG has been able to expand its catchment area to include most of France and Belgium. This kind of intermodal efficiency has not only provided powerful benefits in terms of traffic increase for the airport, but it has also impacted on some network decisions by major airlines. Air France, for instance, has abandoned the Paris-Brussels route, due to the strong cannibalisation effects, in terms of frequency, timing and price, produced by the Thalis high-speed train. Moreover, Lufthansa, when deciding to increase its presence in the French market, has opted for a much-more cost-efficient code-sharing with SNCF (French railways operator) through hubbing at Charles de Gaulle, instead of a much more expensive point-to-point coverage of city pairs. In a broader view, today more than 20 international airlines put their codes on TGV services departing from Charles de Gaulle airport.*

Low-Cost Airports: A Possible Evolutionary Path for Airport Enterprises?

In the air transport environment, the term 'low-cost' is typically related to a specific value proposition in the airline business. It has come to be associated with those providers that reengineer the transport service by eliminating some ancillary services and concentrating on the core benefit with some limited fundamental peripherals only (Holloway, 2003). Low-cost carriers do not offer free-of-charge catering or different service classes, but some of them give rewards to their frequent-fliers, as table 4.1 shows. Moreover, they have to maintain some fundamental peripherals, like ground handling services and minimum seating pitches.

The consequence of this limited service offering is a partial cost saving transfer to customers by means of highly competitive and aggressive fares. This entrepreneurial idea has already gained significant success in some first-tier markets, like North America and the UK, while recent studies predict a brilliant future for them in other market contexts, too. Figure 4.1 shows a predicted evolution of LCCs' market share in the European market, while table 4.2 illustrates LCCs' current market share in some key environments. Figures 4.2 and 4.3 provide evidence concerning the typical features of low-cost carriers compared to traditional, network airlines.

Table 4.1 LCCs providing frequent-flier benefits

Low-cost airline	Own program	Partnership
Air Tran	Yes	
Can Jet	Yes	
Southwest	Yes	
Jet Blue	Yes	
Frontier	Yes	
ATA	Yes	
V-Bird	Yes	
Westjet		Yes
Spirit		Yes
Song		Yes
Ted		Yes
Zip		Yes

Figure 4.1 Projected changes in intra-European passenger market shares, 2000-2010

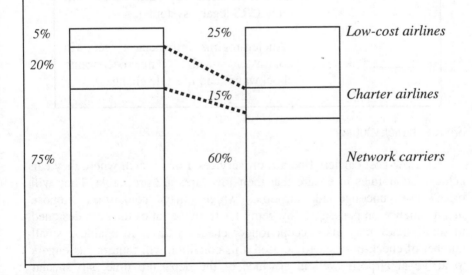

Source: AEA, IATA, Mercer.

Table 4.2 Current LCCs' market shares in some key contexts

Geographic context	Current market share
US	28%
UK	42%
European market (EU boundaries)	9%

Source: OAG timetable.

Figure 4.2 Typical features of network-based airlines

⟹	Massive marketing expenses (advertising, FFPs, travel agents' overrides, network analysis);
⟹	Expensive, fragmented and complex service (classes of tariffs and service, catering, lounges, ground services, etc.);
⟹	Massive use of technology (hard tech: aircraft tailored for each route; soft tech: CRS legacy systems);
⟹	"Ancien-regime" financial targets (in contrast with macroeconomic shockwaves and lifestyle changes).

Source: Jarach, 2004.

Low-cost carriers find airport services a major area where they can achieve economies to ensure that their low fares are profitable. They will often use uncongested airports, which may sometimes impose inconvenience on passengers by being far from the cities they are designed to serve. They may also accept longer check-in times to enable a small number of check-in desks to be used: this condition will require passengers to arrive at airports well in advance of the departure time. No special lounges are provided, resulting in significant cost savings. Finally, the boarding process is a simple one on a 'first come, first served' basis with no pre-allocation of seats (Shaw, 1999).

Figure 4.3   Typical features of low-cost airlines

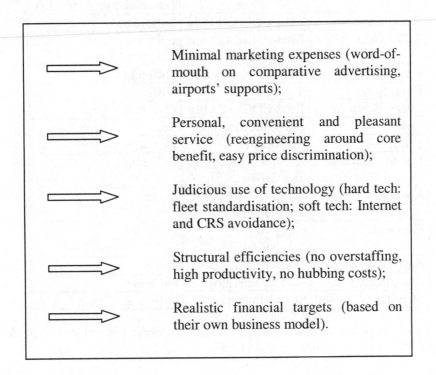

Minimal marketing expenses (word-of-mouth on comparative advertising, airports' supports);

Personal, convenient and pleasant service (reengineering around core benefit, easy price discrimination);

Judicious use of technology (hard tech: fleet standardisation; soft tech: Internet and CRS avoidance);

Structural efficiencies (no overstaffing, high productivity, no hubbing costs);

Realistic financial targets (based on their own business model).

Source: Jarach, 2004.

In the case of airport entities, a widespread diffusion of the low-cost formula requires that all main operational procedures are adapted to the new dominant market trend. This intervention will obviously be required to a greater extent in the case of secondary airports, where LCCs tend to concentrate their traffic and for which LCCs represent their main pipeline customer.

Here, as a strategic answer to the market upsurge of LCCs, it seems possible to propose a new kind of airport positioning: the *low-cost airport*, a highly-specialised market interface designed to satisfy the operational needs of LCCs. Some attempts of this kind can already be seen, for example, London Luton or Brussels Charleroi, where LCCs dominate total airline movements. Table 4.6 illustrates the main European airports that are moving towards a 'low-cost airport' positioning.

Table 4.3 Some examples of European airports with a vocational low-cost positioning

Low-cost airport	Main competitor	Airport authority (same one or different)
Beauvais	Paris CDG and Orly	Different
Milan Orio	Milan Linate and Malpensa	Same*
Charleroi	Brussels National	Different
Carcassone	Toulouse	Different
Cergy-Pontoise	Paris CDG and Orly	Different
Hahn	Frankfurt Main	Same
Liverpool	Manchester	Different
London Luton	London Heathrow and Gatwick	Different
London Stansted	London Heathrow and Gatwick	Same
Prestwick	Glasgow International	Different
Rome Ciampino	Rome Fiumicino	Same
Sandefjord-Torp	Oslo-Gandermoen	Different
Skavsta	Stockholm Arlanda	Different

* SEA, Milan Linate and Malpensa's airport authority, has a 49.9% share in SACBO, Orio's operator.

Source: Graham, 2001.

Typically, LCCs are aggressive in all B2B negotiations. In the case of airports, these players look for economic subsidies to cover start-up costs, cheaper handling, landing and parking fees, plus a significant efficiency in ground operations that will permit short turnaround times. For instance, Ryanair, the European low-cost leader, requires from all of its partner airports a tight 25-minute turnaround time.

These packages of requests often clash with *ancien-regime* and inefficient managerial approaches, that consequently face major difficulties in granting these concessions and affect the profit-related goal of the airport itself.

Thus, the 'low-cost airport' requires, firstly, a significant reduction in the complexity of all organisational levels through a streamlining of hierarchies and functional responsibilities and secondly, an improvement in staff flexibility in the ground operations area has to be achieved.

A greater use of part-time workers may be useful to comply with daily peak-time periods and improve the effectiveness of service to airlines. A significant space will be allocated to self-ticketing and self-check-in kiosks, whilst a constant supervision by ground staff will help passengers in the case of difficulties in performing these operational duties. Some jobs may be lost, but the most important advantage of the airport transformation is that it helps customer airlines to maintain or regain sound productivity advantages. Kiosks may also become an important end customer satisfaction tool when they are integrated into the security process, and can start giving customised information to the passenger about the flight time and also provide real-time information to security staff that will let them react to crowd levels and move staff accordingly.

Finally, in the case of the non-aviation related SBU, low-cost airports will have to adhere to the fact that an average LC passenger tends to spend less at airports than other passenger types.[3] Many market research studies provide evidence which shows declining levels of average expenditure, which is linked to the perception of the 'flight experience' as a pure commodity with almost no psychological involvement. Low-cost airports will thus have to focus their retailing offer on 'impulse goods', like miscellaneous corners, pharmacies, Internet cafés and fast food restaurants, whilst avoiding fashion stores and jewelleries that will be perceived as distant from the passenger's low-cost 'travel concept'.

The Possible Role of Helicopters as a Complementary Feeder and Defeeder of Hub Airports

In the view presented above, airports act as multimodal platforms that manage logistical interchanges of passengers and goods between a combination of complementary transportation solutions: road (private cars, car pooling, taxis, coaches, trucks), rail (commuting and high-speed train services) and sea (ferry services between neighbouring sites).

However, what appears evident is that the forecasted constant increase of primary demand for air services[4] will soon lead to possible

---

[3] This seems to be the case even if the number of business travellers aboard low-cost carriers is constantly increasing. On average, 40% of all low-cost passengers are business travellers.

[4] IATA figures predict an average 5-7% annual increase in air travel demand until 2012.

congestion in multimodal feedering and defeedering and it will lead to delays and problems that could impact on the quality and effectiveness of ground, rail or sea services. Thus, in the case of a small target of high-yield, affluent passengers, a fast way to reach and leave airports could be provided by a massive use of dedicated helicopter shuttle services operating to and from the main centres within the airport's catchment area.

> *An example is the shuttle connection between New York JFK and downtown Manhattan, that has been offered on a complimentary basis to TWA and Pan Am's elite (first and business class) passengers for many years.*

This kind of formula could well be extended beyond the simple airport-to-city commute to connect more distant business locations. A hypothetical example is in the Italian context, where the industrial district of Turin, host of FIAT,[5] could be well-connected with the Milan Malpensa hub, where most of Alitalia's long-haul services are based. This service would be valuable for both Fiat's top managers, as it would significantly cut their total travel times, and for Alitalia, by attracting more high-yield customers and, thus, proactively responding to Lufthansa in the battle for the attraction of connecting traffic at primary hubs.[6] The start-up of helicopter services could, thus, eventually push Alitalia, or other carriers, to code-share and, thereby offer their passengers a smoother and seamless travel journey.

However, the high cost-per-hour of helicopters would probably require financial support from some local institutions to sustain regular shuttle services and maintain an accessible fare level, a major example being provided by Monte Carlo-Nice helishuttle, which is partly subsidised by Monaco.

In this case, the helicopter service is included in a broader place marketing project, aimed at attracting new business and industrial investment in certain territories by improving the quality of overall transportation connections.

> *Macao, formerly a Portuguese colony, returned to China in 1999. It is a special administrative region of just 500,000 people but it is strategically located near the so-called Special Economic Zone and near Hong Kong. Its main attraction, besides its scenic beauty, combining Eastern and*

---

[5] Fiat is a worldwide car manufacturer and a large private Italian company.

[6] Recently Lufthansa has increased the number of frequencies between Turin and Frankfurt and Munich to catch a larger slice of high-yield connecting traffic originating in the Turin area.

Latin architectures, is the casinos. The new airport was completed in 1995 and is now managed by a private company, owned by the local government and by the gambling society. Macao airport is the main base of east Asia Airlines, that has a fleet of three Sikorsky S76-C helicopters for 12 passengers, which fly from Macao to Shun Tak Centre in Hong Kong, and also have three flights each day to Shenzhen.

Airport Revenue Management

In the air transportation business, revenue management has been mostly associated with hyper discrimination of pricing tariffs made by airlines. In recent times, this technique has come to be applied by car rental companies, and also widely extended to hotel chains.

Nowadays, revenue management software permits the operator to produce a bundle of different pricing options for each target cluster. On the one hand, higher tariffs will be linked to maximum flexibility levels for the passenger that will allow travellers to change both his travel paths and airline service. Cheaper tariffs will be offered in exchange for significant flexibility reductions, a typical example being provided by the application of the so-called 'Sunday rule'.[7]

However, this kind of demand-oriented pricing approach may be extended to other zones of proximity within the air transport value chain. One of these could be represented by the airport environment. Thus, we may speak of the application of airport revenue management in the case of price discrimination for airport lounges, parking, handling and landing fees.

All these activities share a common problem in terms of rigid capacity levels, at least in the short-to-medium term.[8] Also significant load factors fluctuations within the timing unit considered, be it a day, week, month or an IATA season. The application of airport revenue management may permit the achievement of higher load factors during off-peak periods through the use of highly appealing discounted fares as a form of market stimulation.

In the case of airport parking, for instance, lower levels of space occupation is usual at nights or weekends. This problem could be successfully dealt with by including discounted fees in a tour package offered to leisure travellers, with different levels of promotional capacity in

---

[7] Usually if a customer accepts to stay at a destination for a Saturday night, the fare will be much cheaper than a standard one. This kind of price policy is usually targeted at leisure clusters.

[8] In the long term, capacity upgrades may be put into practice, as in the case of terminal expansion.

the case of peak or off-peak seasons. Some form of price stimulation could also be created as an ancillary package to support the non-aviation business of an airport enterprise. Geneva is a good example of this practice. Here airport managers have improved the power of attraction of their in-terminal supermarket by granting the first hour of parking for free. This approach could be suitable even in the case of other businesses, like, for instance, joint promotion activities to attract new customers at the airport's restaurants and food courts.

A similar *modus operandi* seems possible for airport lounges. It's common practice for airlines to pay a standard fee for every passenger entering an airport's lounge. As flights tend to occur in waves of incoming and departing passengers, even lounges will face variance in their levels of occupation. The lounge operator could exploit the revenue management tool to attract extra traffic during off-peak periods, eventually extending to other clusters of passengers the chance to rest at the lounge, rather than solely relying on business travellers.

> *BAA acts in a similar way at Stansted. This airport is home to many low-cost carriers that do not provide any sort of extra benefit, like lounge access, to their customers. BAA offers all passengers a chance to enter the lounge by paying a standard fee. The same fee however is charged throughout the day. A chance for revenue growth by the airport authority could come from the application of the above mentioned discrimination policy.*

Revenue management could also be applied to ramp and ground handling services. In the case of hub airports, for instance, ground operations during flight waves are mostly saturated, whilst some spare capacity is available at off-peak times. Thus, a different level of discounted policy, aimed at attracting point-to-point carriers during off-peak times, could be a rationale means of improving the cost efficiency of the ground handler, whilst it could also be conceivable to introduce a rise in price during rush hours to improve the overall hub efficiency.

This kind of approach could be studied also for landing fees and ATC services. In this case, however, it should be managed by public bodies at national or supranational levels rather than on a single airport basis. This would be essential to avoid conflicts between private operator concerns and the need to provide public and neutral services to all intermediate operators involved.

All examples presented here refer to the application of price discrimination and revenue management to the airport business. The passage from concept to implementation of revenue management, by means of complex and dedicated softwares, both multiplies the range of tariffs available and creates those information asymmetries that may actually contribute to improve the airport's economic viability.

Airport Alliances

Since the 1980s, one of the most fashionable tools used to reinforce firms' market presence has been through alliance paths within industry boundaries (horizontal alliances) or by including companies from related sectors, as in the case of value chain or cross-industry alliances (Jarach, 1998).

These co-evolutionary designs, implemented in equity-based or non-equity contractual agreements, may be able to assure partners a bundle of competitive and commercial opportunities. Moreover, through alliances a number of strategic and operational goals can be achieved much faster than in the case of a purely internal approach. The latter needing much more time and resources and also the absence of some institutional barriers (Doz and Hamel, 1998).

Some of the obvious benefits that alliances have proven to create for the partners involved are:

- a dramatic cut in both the scope of financial support needed and in the level of risk compared to a stand-alone situation;
- a mutual sharing of operational and marketing costs associated with the business venture;
- a chance to enter or have better coverage of some value-adding markets and demand clusters, especially in the case of tight regulatory regimes that limit the sharing of capacity (as is the case in the air transport industry);
- the evolution of the behavioural patterns of the industry, from a publicly-regulated monopoly or oligopoly to a players-driven industry. In this case, some acceptable forms[9] of trust may enable players to achieve higher returns on investments (higher incomes and lower costs) that are, once again, a consequence of lower levels of competitive intensity.

In the aviation world, the start-up of some bilateral agreements between actors, like in the case of airlines, can be traced back to the 1960s. These types of partnership were basically operational ones, whose

---

[9] Typically granted through an anti-trust immunity by governing bodies.

implementation took the form of interline and pro-rata agreements under the IATA umbrella (Jarach, 1998 and 1999).

The strategic need to achieve higher concentration levels in what can be described as a historically fragmented context has been growing since the 1990s. Since then the first 'airline constellations' have debuted on the market, i.e. Star, Skyteam and Oneworld. Table 4.7 outlines the main airline carriers that are included in the top three constellations.

In the case of airports, high fragmentation of ruling power between various stakeholders, most of them part of the public sector, has made industry players think and act purely on the basis of a local and individualistic approach for a long time. Despite the many good reasons to collaborate, most organisations have failed for decades to take full advantage of their opportunities to do so. In many cases the frictional costs outweigh the obvious benefits. These costs include managerial time and effort; concerns about priorities and deliveries, incompatibility of IT systems and strategies and other administrative headaches that raise the cost of collaboration (Pralahad and Ramaswamy, 2004). Only in very recent times, some best-in-class actors have identified a need for cooperation as a main driver for gaining or improving an international visibility.

> *One of the best examples concerning an attempt for a multinational airport alliance is 'Pantares'. This partnership, which has never actually taken off, involves Amsterdam, Frankfurt and Rome airport authorities. Another case is provided by Worldairports, its partners being Aeroports de Paris, Copenhagen, Dallas-Ft.Worth, Houston and BAA Group, with the goal of creating a shared e-business platform with both B2B and B2C interfaces. Concerning local patterns of integration, the Italian context provides a good example. Aeroporti Holding, which has as one of its major stakeholders the Benetton Group, now controls stakes in the airport authorities of Turin and Florence and aims to establish a national conglomerate of regional entities.*

The main goal of airport alliances lies in the search for stronger negotiating power within the air transport value chain to effectively counteract the central position of airlines. In fact, airports position looks weaker than in the recent past, due to the creation of airline alliances.

Moreover, airport alliances strive to increase partner power in B2B relationships with some 'soft provider' suppliers, like catering or retailing companies, for instance.

Table 4.4 The main airline constellations of alliances

Brand name	First tier carriers	Other associated airlines
Star	Lufthansa, United Airlines	SAS, Thai, Air Canada, Varig, Singapore Airlines, Air New Zealand, British Midland, ANA, AUA Group, LOT, Asiana, TAP
Oneworld	American Airlines, British Airways	Qantas, Cathay Pacific, LAN Chile, Finnair, Iberia
Skyteam	Air France, Delta Airlines	Korean Air, Alitalia, Aeromexico, CSA, KLM, Northwest, Continental, Aeroflot, Air Europa, Air Malta[10]

Source: Author's search.

We may, thus, try to split the main types of airport partnerships into three categories: point-to-point alliances, multi-point alliances and management contract alliances.

Point-to-Point Alliances

The origin of this partnership, which can be either non-equity or equity-based, lies in cooperation practices between a pair of airports, not necessarily located in the same or close markets.

The range of partnerships may involve a bundle of managerial issues, from jointly handling production to joint purchases of airport retailing goods or below-the-line operational support of airport practices. The latter refers to a temporary transfer of managers, employees or machines to the partner, particularly in the case of different peaks of each one's business, or support in the provision of specific knowledge

---

[10] Aeroflot, Air Europa and Air Malta have expressed their wish to enter Skyteam and acceptance audits are apparently under way.

concerning IT solutions or qualified skills related to crisis management procedures.

Of course, the broader the partnership, the greater the number of functions and departments that tend to be involved. And when the cooperation becomes tight, a natural step is the transformation of it from a purely contractual one to an equity-based formula or a full merger of airport enterprises.

These partnerships can be built on a mono or multi-brand formula; in the former case, a single umbrella branding will be created; in the latter case, each player will maintain its corporate identity in the market.

Multi-Point Alliances

The multi-point co-evolutionary view involves a significant stretching of the dimensional boundaries of the alliance.

Here a panel of airport operators choose to sign a cooperation agreement, which can be equity based or non-equity based, to include expertise sharing on some functions or on the whole package of operations. Airports will be able to choose a single brand, like in the case of the trilateral alliance branded as Pantares, or maintain a stand-alone positioning.

The strategic goal of this multi-point agreement lies not only in the dimensions of critical mass which can be used in negotiations, but also in the stronger lobbying power that partners may put into practice when relating with some supranational 'metaregulators'.

On the one hand, the participation of a bundle of actors from different geographic contexts may create some growing complexities and increase the costs of coordination between partners. This situation will need higher cooperative competences within the alliances; these being resident inside the alliance-leader[11] or split between the various partners.

On the other hand, this partnership may be positively associated with increasing numbers of traffic movements between partners. This condition may be positively exacerbated in the case of mono-brand alliances that can achieve higher visibility in both B2B and B2C negotiations.

---

[11] The alliance-leader could either be the founder of the multi-point alliance or the main player in terms of movements and passengers.

Management Contract

A final form of partnership for the airport business deals with the so called 'management contract'. Here no ownership clauses are involved and the agreement usually occurs between a government and a private subject.[12]

The contractor takes responsibility for the day-to-day operation of the airport and agrees to pay an annual management fee, usually related to the performance of the airport. Investment will normally remain the responsibility of the government owner and so the overall economic risk will be shared between the owner and the management company. For the government owner this may be politically more acceptable, whereas for the contractor such an arrangement may be attractive in countries where greater financial exposure may be seen as too great a risk (Graham, 2001).

> *For instance, AENA, the Spanish airport operator, has management contracts for Cayo Coco airport in Cuba and three major airports in Colombia, whilst ADP has management contracts in Cameroon and Madagascar.*

This kind of agreement may, thus be beneficial for both parties. On a short-term view, the government will see the economic potential of its airports maximised, thanks to the competences of the contractor.

In a longer-term perspective, the government involved will also be able to improve the local knowledge of airport management in its own infrastructures, with a chance of cross-cultural fertilisation of management practices by the contractor and, eventually, a possible return to a stand-alone perspective.

The contractor, instead, will be using this approach to enter highly regulated and blocked countries, where foreign direct investments are not allowed. This path will also permit the contractor to scout the local market and establish a 'commercial antenna', with a future possible decision to shift to a direct investment if local limitations are removed.

---

[12] Which, in any case, could be public-owned, too.

Chapter 5

The Development of the Non Aviation-Related Value Proposition

Towards an Evolution of the 'Traditional Airport' Business Model

Every industry facing new 'rules of the game' sees its more proactive actors differentiating their own value proposition to avoid the risk of service commoditisation and, as a consequence, virulent market cannibalization (Levitt, 1980).

Until recently, however, this kind of approach hasn't been perceived as a top priority by airport managers. In fact, in the past, the airport business looked to be quite simple to manage. Like in many other static market environments, success was defined by only a few basic indicators. In the case of airports, the most important figure was traffic increase, either on the passenger or on the cargo side, to be matched with IATA average industry forecasts.[1] In the short term, achieving this goal meant more revenues, in the form of increased passenger taxes as well as landing and handling fees from the core aviation-related business. In a longer-view perspective a wider level of activity would create a chance for the airport infrastructure to be upgraded, gain higher political visibility for airport managers and create stronger consensus among local stakeholders, due to the creation of new job opportunities for local communities.

At the same time, airports didn't have to worry too much about controlling their own operating costs. On the one hand, high barriers to competition, in terms of the number of players allowed, meant cost increases could be relatively easily passed over to customers. On the other hand, spatial upgrades to cope with primary demand increases were almost completely financed by the State or regional/local entities in the form of huge subsidies, with the aim of improving the effectiveness of the country's overall infrastructural package.

---

[1] For example, if IATA's was forecasting a 7% annual traffic increase, it was sufficient for airport managers to match this, with no commitment to achieve a stronger performance.

Thus, we may say that airports were acting as a logistics medium, but seldom as a real business, to satisfy the undifferentiated air transportation needs of its catchment area, as a point of access and facilitation between airline services and demand clusters. Political diktats and the generation of consensus within the airport's administrative catchment area were much more significant for airport managers than pure P&L figures (Jarach, 2001).

Unfortunately for airports, however, fundamental shifts in the business environment are rapidly changing the 'rules of the game' and dramatically impacting on the industry's traditional success formulas, making the afore mentioned strategy frameworks almost obsolete.

Third-party, non-airport handlers, like Aviapartner, Mensies, Swissport and Globeground are expanding on a global scale and entering new market arenas with price-cutting strategies that often cannot be matched by existing airport handling monopolies.

In other words, value generation for airports is no longer linked to traditional core functions, but much more with managerial ingenuity in seizing new strategic and market opportunities. Failure to anticipate changes in the marketplace can leave players with business models tailored for markets that no longer exist facing the danger of marginalisation from the market. Figure 5.1 shows in detail the path towards diversification of value propositions in the airport business, a subject that will be further analysed in the next section.

New Evolutionary Patterns for Airport Enterprises

The traditional airport managerial approach mentioned above had previously underestimated the relevance of a vast category of secondary activities within their own airport boundaries.

These may, in fact, play a significant role in complementing and supporting the primary service of the airport infrastructure and become a major source of airport revenues.

In the case of a 'traditional airport' approach, a dominant focus on aviation-related activities meant revenues could rise or decline according, firstly, to macroeconomic and environmental changes, like:

- the pace of economic cycles;
- the break-out of international crises and wars;
- exchange-rate and crude oil fluctuations.

All these elements appear well beyond the scope of prediction or control of airport managements.

Secondly, traffic and, consequently, revenue modifications had to be correlated with micro-environmental, industry-specific patterns of action. We may mention some positive factors, like the introduction of new routes and frequencies related to the entry of new carriers, or negative events, like airline failures or carriers' cost-cutting measures.

Figure 5.1 The diversification of the airport value proposition

MANY	**Service focused**
	
	(for instance, airports
	  serving all categories
	  of carriers)
		Aggresively diversified
		targeting primary and
		and secondary
		catchment areas in a
		wider and creative
		way

NUMBER OF SERVED CLUSTERS	**Focused on a single positioning** (for instance, low-cost airports)	**Diversified,** but targeting the the primary catchment area only
FEW		

NARROW   WIDE
RANGE OF AIRPORT'S VALUE PROPOSITION

Source: Jarach, 2002.

Unfortunately, even a rather proactive airport authority can only have a modest influence over these kind of drivers, not to mention the ratio between business and leisure passengers or the seasonal mix between scheduled and charter carriers. For instance, by means of costly marketing efforts, in the form of huge subsidies, airport managers may succeed in attracting carriers to add new routes or frequencies to the current timetable.

However, evidence from the past has clearly demonstrated that these efforts may generate only a modest impact on airports' long-term traffic patterns. It is fair to say that the greatest stimulus for traffic may instead occur when carriers simply respond to perceived passenger primary demand, which is connected to the economic wealth or leisure attractiveness of the area in which the airport is located (Hanlon, 1996; Valdani and Jarach, 1997).

Summing up, an airport management may, thus, strive to stimulate traffic demand, in conjunction with the efforts of carriers, but would certainly not succeed in impacting and modifying the economic macro-fundamentals of its own catchment area.

A proactive and visionary airport management may gain a significant degree of entrepreneurial freedom when aiming to increase its overall revenues and profits by focusing on its non-aviation business side.

This second path provides for airport differentiation in terms of the range of in-house services the site decides to offer the target audience, consistent with the positioning target already chosen. This option tries to increase the strategic weight of the airport infrastructure on the market as a 'multi-service provider' and appears more likely to regain some monopolistic rents within a highly competitive environment. (Levitt, 1969; Kotler and Scott, 1997).

In fact, if compared with most other industries, airports enjoy unique opportunities for gaining extra profits from non-aviation operations, thanks to a high degree of strategic control, primarily in the form of physical 'customer ownership'. Airports have a customer base that any high-street retailer would willingly exchange body parts for and, furthermore, these customers are a trapped audience. This happens because airport customers tend to spend a good deal of time within the terminal walls because they are forced to do so by the range and profile of operations to be undertaken in an airport infrastructure before the flight boarding.

Air passengers will often arrive at the terminal building well before the scheduled departure time, especially if flying to sunshine destinations with a charter carrier and be submitted to a series of operational duties and security controls. Also passengers' meeters and greeters will be waiting for a long time at the airport, especially when incoming or departing flights have been delayed, and employees of the various players in the value chain will spend most of their day working inside the airport perimeter and will look for a variety of service propositions to satisfy their primary needs. Eventually, citizens inside the airport's catchment area will tend to stay in the terminal building for long periods of time to help justify the trip from downtown, especially when the airport's value proposition looks innovative and unique when compared with neighbouring outlets.

The relatively long duration of a customer's stay within the 'shopping mall with runaways' may have the following consequence: a direct and rather positive impact on the average income of each shopping outlet and service provider hosted in the terminal, as customers may choose to spend some of their spare time shopping.

This purchase intention may become very significant in terms of the magnitude of economic figures, however, airports have not only to put passengers in the right state of mind to shop, but also give them a reason to shop.

In this sense, airport management, given a terminal's space constraints, will have to attract a range of offerings tailored to the specific characteristics of the target demand with plenty of variety in terms of depth and breadth of products and services available. At this stage, a detailed knowledge of the buying behaviour and requirements of the different clusters of customers is extremely helpful in driving the airport management to choose the right outlets within the terminal and gaining customers' preference (Jarach, 2002).

Figure 5.2 illustrates the passage from the traditional view of airport operations to the new and fascinating formula of 'shopping mall with runways' with a high degree of service diversification and marketing ingenuity and creativity.

The 'Commercial Airport' Philosophy: A New Perspective

A 'commercial airport' exhibits critical differences both in its strategic mission and in its inherent marketing implementation, when compared to the 'traditional airport' concept (Levitt, 1969 and 1980; Lovelock, 1984; Berry, 1986; Jarach, 2001).

This new market formula sees airport infrastructures evolving from pure mono or multimodal logistical medum into more sophisticated market entities that may be described as a 'multipoint service-provider firms'.

Thus, apart from its conservative, traditional air-side business, airports also tend to become commercial hubs, in which a bundle of diversified service propositions and products are offered to an enlarged category of target customers (Doganis, 1992). This new set of potential customers includes not only air passengers and air transportation employees, but also local-communities residents, firms and firms' employees operating inside the airport's catchment area, tourists and aviation enthusiasts.

Figure 5.2   The enriched service package offered by a modern airport enterprise

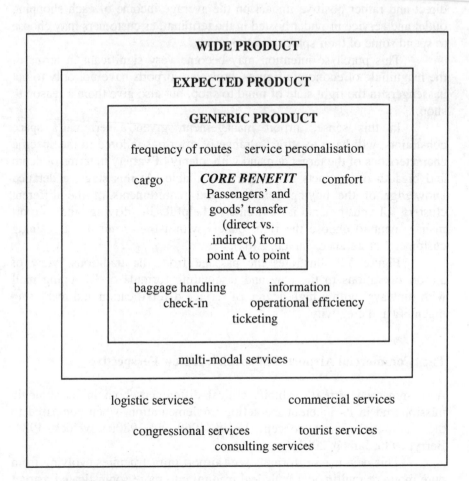

WIDE PRODUCT

EXPECTED PRODUCT

GENERIC PRODUCT

frequency of routes   service personalisation

cargo   *CORE BENEFIT*   comfort
Passengers' and
goods' transfer
(direct vs.
indirect) from
point A to point

baggage handling   information
check-in   operational efficiency
ticketing

multi-modal services

logistic services   commercial services

congressional services   tourist services
consulting services

Source: Jarach, 2001.

The same recent increase in competition between airports in the aviation-related business, especially when dealing with primary hubs, plays an important role in the development of the 'commercial airport'. In other words, we will not assist the transformation of airports acting like commercial districts and without aircraft movements. But, in the near future, neither will we assist to airports that will able to survive on aviation-related business only and, thus, will have clear financial problems.

A primary reason for a passenger – especially in the case of a price-inelastic frequent-flyer – to choose an airport is clearly linked to the type, quality and quantity of airline services operated, or to the favourable location of the complex and its close position to the place of origin or destination. In this case an evaluation of non-aviation related activities will play a secondary role. However, growing numbers of passengers may be instead influenced, in their hubbing decisions, by means of a rich package of commercial facilities, a hypothesis that today is much more frequent than one may perceive. This is most true in the case of destinations served by hubs located close to one another and with overlapping catchment areas.

> *For instance, some hubs in the Middle East, like Abu Dhabi, Bahrain and Dubai, all have similarities in the type of destinations served and compete by emphasizing their non-aviation related commercial offer. They also organise regular lotteries for airport shoppers to reward their purchasing loyalty.*

According to this approach, five new areas of activity may be identified, as a complement of the traditional core business, when dealing with the 'commercial airport' approach:

- commercial services;
- tourist services;
- conference services;
- logistic and property management services;
- consulting services.

Commercial Services (Airport Retailing)

In this broad micro-category, practitioners usually include all airport retailing activities. These are the vast package of commercial ventures offering products and services aimed at satisfying customers' needs, mainly impulse ones.

From a demand side, we may identify five major target-demand clusters for commercial services:

- a basically captive audience, consisting of traditional origin, destination and transit passengers: this cluster is mainly driven to shop for primary needs' items or to purchase a gift for family or friends;

- the so called 'meeters and greeters', coming to airports to accompany or pick-up Visiting Friends and Relatives (VFR), travellers or job-related contacts. These could be attracted to spend some of their own spare time at the airport shopping or eating;
- an airport enterprise's, airlines' and other service providers' employees within the air transport value chain: they are typically purchasers of commercial services either for their work or private needs;
- local residents around the airport or close to it;
- companies within the airport's catchment area: they are potentially a target of B2B services in the logistic and property management area.

There is a widespread consensus that most, if not all, of the airport retailing offer will see a departing passenger as a logical and rather unique cluster of demand.

In fact, the airport retailing formula may prove to be very popular for local residents, meeters and greeters, companies and the air transport value chain's employees. This happens, for instance, when some legal restrictions on opening hours of downtown retailers are in place, and the airport commercial offer, instead, can be accessed on a 24-hour basis or, at least, on an extended daily opening time basis.

Moreover, when a package of mass transportation services between the main city centre and the airport itself is available, city residents may decide to take shopping trips to the airport, extending the scope of coverage of the airport retailing formula well outside the traditional airline passenger focus.

This latter case is provided by Amsterdam Schiphol airport. Back in 1995, the Dutch hub opened a landside commercial facility named 'Schiphol Plaza', with more than 400 shops on 5.400 square meters. This venue is easily accessible to a vast customer audience, thanks to the great number of road and rail connections that link Schiphol with the city centres within its own catchment area. Another good example comes from Naples airport in Italy, where the projected construction of a subway line between the airport and downtown should greatly improve the visibility of the terminal's commercial venues.

Eventually, an enriched power of attraction for the airport retailing facilities might be provided by a differentiation of its own retailing mix. This goal is achieved by innovation in the service formats that are within an airport's boundaries, or by reengineering the existing bundle of commercial venues in a new and highly emotional environment, taking as a benchmark the example provided by theme parks.

> *The new Seoul's Incheon airport is well known by travellers and local residents for the number of saunas and fitness centres that have been put within the terminal's walls.*

From the offer side, we may pool all in-airport commercial ventures within three main groups:

- *commercial services in a strict sense*, which include those services that are closely linked to the more traditional and conservative airport-retailing offer. Major examples are provided by fashion boutiques, jewellers,[2] tobacco retailers, newsstands, car rentals, money changers;
- *food and beverage services*, like traditional restaurants, fast foods, bars and snack-bars;

> *Food and beverage is usually considered one of the first businesses which attracts a managers' attention when dealing with the goal of capturing 'non-passengers' demand for airports. However, getting consumers to these points of sale is not as easy a task as one may think at first glance. In this sense, a good example can be provided by looking at what happened at 'Encounters', a pub-restaurant located at Los Angeles International airport. This facility, which actually has with no connecting passages with any terminal in the airport complex, had faced serious financial problems in the past, as it was not getting sufficient return on investment for its shareholders and, indirectly, for the airport as a whole. A search for alternatives led the airport authority to contact Disney Corporation and get a reengineered layout for the restaurant which would include a new service concept. Now visitors can have their dinner close to a spectacular view of aircraft taking off and landing at LAX. This situation gives 'Encounters' a significant competitive advantage over its own direct competitors outside the airport.*
> *In Europe, London Gatwick has been particularly successful. Between 1992 and 1994, the airport has increased its food and beverage revenues by 70%. During this period, the number of operators grew from 4 to 18 and the number of outlets increased from 7 to 24. In the Gatwick Village landside section of the South Terminal, there are a number of standalone restaurants such as McDonald's and Garfunkel's, as well as several smaller outlets grouped around a viewing food court.*

---

[2] Usually direct heirs of duty-free shops, where these facilities can no longer work.

- *complementary services*, this category deals with services not historically included in an airport retailing mix and, thus, representing a major source of differentiation. For instance, ATMs, religious services, local gourmet shops, miscellaneous corners, Internet cafés, pharmacies, florists, fitness and wellness centres, pharmacies, hairdressers, hotel and info points, merchandising kiosks;

Somebody at first glance could think of a hairdressers as a highly inconsistent business within an airport's value proposition. Empirical evidence, instead, shows this venue is highly profitable, as in the case of Vienna International airport. In fact, airport hairdressers can count on a captive audience consisting of airport and airline employees all spending many hours in the terminal walls. This condition has a positive effect in smoothing off-peak periods for this service, maximising the return on investment and profitability, once again, for the airport enterprise.

Hotel points are basically kiosks located in the landside arrival area offering customers a chance to book and stay at one of the catchment area's hotels. These encounters often offer an enriched bundle of services, by also selling, for instance, hotel stays together with a limousine or a shuttle service to drive a customer directly to the chosen hotel.

Info points usually take the form of some kind of kiosk, located in the landside arrival area, where you can get information about how to reach a certain location, usually a tourist site, by mass transportation, or where brochures and leaflets concerning promotional activities are available.

Miscellaneous corners are a typical British value proposition. Usually located in the landside arrival area, these shops are open for a long period of the day and offer passengers and customers a chance to purchase basic items, like drinks, newspapers, OTC drugs, sandwiches, and so on. They look like a good solution especially when terminal constraints do not allow hosting a number of single specialised shops, as in the case of London City Airport.

- *advertising services*, linked to the commercial exploitation of spaces within the terminal boundaries to promote sales of various products and brands.

Airport enterprises have not historically been either active or creative actors when dealing with the exploitation of commercial opportunities from advertising, notwithstanding that airports are an ideal place for advertising. Millions of people pass through the terminal buildings every

year and their level of attention is highly sought after. Moreover, there
are a lot of different chances to catch customers' attention for commercial
purposes, for instance, at check-in procedures, before boarding, at
baggage carousels in the arrival lounges, and so on. New opportunities
are being offered by some technological innovations. A good example is
represented by Lufthansa System's 'Trolley Man'. This is a computerized
system that can be installed on individual baggage trolleys. A transmitter
will permit the trolley manager to know the exact location of the
passenger in the terminal building. This valuable commercial information
can be used to automatically activate rolling banners inside the terminal.
So, when the passenger approaches the banner, it will start to show an
advertising message, that can be tailored to the kind of needs a passenger
is presumed to have in that moment. The 'Trolley Man' system is now
being used at Dubai, Singapore and Newark airports.

Aiming to maximise profit generation by means of royalties, airport
enterprises will have to place each concessionaire in the right location to
facilitate the offer-demand matching in a consistent way.

First of all, multi-terminal airports may have significantly different
target audiences, implying that a different retailing offer will have to be
developed for each individual terminal.

Half of Heathrow's Terminal 1 passengers are travelling on business and
well over half are men. There is therefore a significant number of retailers
that are geared towards this market: Austin Reid, Thomas Pink and Tie
Rack (fashion); Links of London (accessories); and Whiskies of the World.
There are also important differences between scheduled and charter
flights, as a review of retailing between, for example, Heathrow Terminal
4 and Gatwick South Terminal would reveal. The former is geared
towards business purchasers, whilst the latter has more holiday-related
items (leisure travellers purchase more electronics and confectionery than
business travellers). Charter passengers tend also to arrive earlier and
have a longer dwell time. Data from Milan's two airports demonstrate
that the average dwell time at the business-oriented Lineate is 99 minutes,
compared to 131 minutes at Malpensa's leisure-oriented Terminal 2.

Evidence from best-in-class operators shows that some value
propositions have to be located in the landside departing hall to benefit
from combined movements of passengers, citizens, air transport employees
and meeters. Other points of sales, however, will require being as close as
possible to boarding gates, targeting only the departing passenger cluster.
Some retailers will achieve their best commercial potential when located in
the landside arrival lounge to satisfy, once again, a varied target of
consumers. In the case of European airports, there is also a need to split

shops' location between Schengen and Extra-Schengen areas of the airport. For instance, in the case of a hub airport, jewellers and fashion boutiques will be better placed in the Extra-Schengen areas, where the target audience typically consists of long-haul and transit flyers. Here this retailing offer tends to have both higher penetration rates (the proportion of passengers who actually spend)[3] and higher expenditures per passenger[4] (Humphries, 1996).

Figure 5.3 illustrates some examples of useful empirical correlations between various types of sales points and the areas of the terminal building in which to locate these commercial activities.

Figure 5.3 Ideal placement of outlets and services within a terminal: airside vs. landside areas

Departure hall landside	Departure hall airside	Arrival hall
Gourmet shop	Duty-free shops	Pharmacy
Bars/restaurants/food court	Bars/restaurants	Bars/restaurants
Hairdresser	Last minute duty-free shop	Info point
Thematic shops (*related to the distinctive products of the catchment area*)	Jeweller	Hotel point
Fashion stores	Money changer	Bank
News-stand		Miscellaneous
		Florist
		Car rental

Source: Jarach, 2002.

The aforementioned bundle of commercial practices represents today the main component of non-aviation related activities. In this sense, there is also some managerial literature about airport management that tends to match the concept of airport retailing with the non-aviation business. This explains why the 'shopping mall with runaways' idea is now

---

[3] This should be quite obvious, as only 'ticketed customers' have access to airside areas. In contrast, landside has a much higher potential coverage, as its power of attraction is exercised over a wider spectrum of clusters.

[4] This will also be highly influenced by the profile of the main airline at that airport, as some carriers, like British Airways or Lufthansa, typically capture richer traffics than ones managed by Latin European carriers.

being implemented in many primary hubs and regional airports, especially in the European context. In this sense, imitation from intra-industry competitors will naturally tend, in the short-to-medium term, to lower the distinctive power of attraction generated by the pioneer airport managements, reducing consistently, *rebus sic stantibus*, the economic relevance of its commercial catchment area.

That's why airports aiming to stay at the industry's competitive edge have to search for new innovative tools to realise the scope for further perceived market advantage by the customer. Airport retailing, in fact, is just one of the many ingredients that can permit the 'commercial airport' business concept to succeed in the market. Thus, we strongly believe that there is a need to extend the concept of non-aviation related activities well beyond this conservative view. In other words, non-aviation practices must now deal with all those forms of revenue generation that come from the exploitation of airport platforms for purposes not correlated with technical support of aircraft and passengers.

Moreover, it's very clear that the airport environment, when exploited in a creative way, may become a location with unique features not only for shopping, but also for many other ancillary services that may give way to high emotional rather than value-added impact. Thus, strengthening the view of the non-aviation related business to other sources of activity can be a good stimulus for creativity and innovation by proactive airport managements. In this sense, the non-aviation related business unit grows to include all sources of activity by means of a different concept of airport service and value proposition.

Tourist Services

The 'airport as a tourism and leisure destination' concept provides the need for creative marketing strategies to attract additional influxes of demand, not just those who have airline tickets. In other words, airport-enterprises may also sell a new form of entertainment, capable of generating autonomous interest in a broad audience, thanks to a rather unique consumption experience. Spotters and aviation enthusiasts are a logical first target for this approach. For instance, London Heathrow airport and Munich airport some years ago launched specific spaces, like terraces and artificial hills, access to which is regulated by an entrance fee thus providing a significant source of additional revenues. This can be contrasted with the case, for instance, in most Italian airports, where spotters are still prevented from accessing good viewing areas for security and military reasons that clearly conflict with this 'airport as a tourist location' approach.

> *Viewing facilities are second to none at Birmingham airport. The Aviation Experience is a large enclosed terrace giving views of arriving and departing aircraft together with multimedia and fully interactive display screens connected to remote cameras around the airfield, allowing visitors to zoom in on individual aircraft and follow them around. Other displays give information on the aircraft types which can be seen and there is also a quiz game to test your knowledge. An indoor viewing area is located above Terminal 1 with access via a lift from the front of the building or from the first floor adjacent to the departure lounge entrance. Completing the picture, Ian Allen has a bookshop within the Aviation Experience, stocked with everything from books to models, prints and viewing equipment to cater for all tourists' aviation needs.*

Some airports have become 'event organisers' to stimulate complementary demand in daily or yearly off-peak periods. This goal has been achieved through radical innovation in the value proposition. Frankfurt airport opened a discothèque[5] inside the Terminal building, this best-practice being rapidly benchmarked and imitated by Munich airport, too. Amsterdam Schiphol has launched a casino in the transit area, as have Frankfurt and Munich airports, while Milan Malpensa airport, has hosted music concerts inside the new Terminal 1 on an ad-hoc basis. Many airports have built golf courses inside or close to their boundaries, targeting this highly-affluent cluster. For instance, Dallas-Forth Worth and Auckland airports have a golf course just outside their boundaries and organise dedicated caddy transfers for golf lovers. But the best example comes from Thailand, where Bangkok airport hosts a golf course between its two operating runways!

> *An extreme case is provided by Kuala Lumpur's Sepang airport in Malaysia. This infrastructure has been built within the Gateway Park, where aircraft movements occur every day close to a bundle of tourist activities. This Park has been divided into three zones, each one with a different environment. One area hosts a Formula 1 circuit, while other ones include a jeep safari tour, a golf course, a fishing pier and a shooting perimeter, with more attractions coming shortly.*

Art exhibitions are being organised by many airports, too, not necessarily only primary hubs. In the case of art exhibitions, the goal of airport management can be threefold. First, the creation of a cultural event

---

[5] Apparently, this has now been closed.

stimulates local residents to come into the terminal complex, which helps narrow the historical and rather conflicting relationships between the infrastructure and neighbouring communities. Second, this increasing movement of people can improve the average income of airport retailing shops. In this case, airport managers will have to locate the art exhibition where fewer transit movements occur. This decision, thus, may clearly upgrade the number and quality of commercial and shopping contacts. Eventually, the airport's decision to host such an event may produce a significant and direct economic return, thanks to dedicated sponsorship activities dealing with this cultural event.

The relevance of this service diversification, in terms of direct and related additional inflows of income, is fairly obvious: for instance, enthusiasts, disco-lovers and gamblers have the potential to generate demand for retailing and food services. Figure 5.4, on a purely speculative basis, tries to quantify the magnitude of direct and indirect revenues arising from the start-up of a new tourist service.

Figure 5.4 Potential revenues arising from the opening of a discotheque in an airport complex

Direct income	
Opening time of the venue	365 dd./y.
Daily disco customers	200
Price of ticket	13 Euro
Revenues	949.000 Euro
Indirect income	
Parking	
(4 customers per car, 4 hrs. stop, hr. rate 4 euro)	365.000 Euro
Restaurants	
(fast-food, average expense per person 6 Euro)	438.000 Euro
Shopping	
(average expense 10 Euro, target 40% of disco's customers)	292.000 Euro
Terrace on aircraft flight operations	
(price 3 Euro, target 5% of disco's customers)	10.950 Euro
royalties on shopping, parking, food and discotheque	15%
royalties on terrace (directly managed)	100%
Estimation of revenues for the airport authority	
from the opening of the discotheque	**317.550 Euro**

Source: Jarach, 2002.

Conference Services

Other areas of market interest for commercially-minded airports may arise from the conference market. This potentially high-yield cluster is looking for the availability of large and spacious areas in which to host delegates and plan meetings with the support of state-of-the-art technological devices, throughout the year.

The airport site may experience two sources of competitive advantage over other nearby conference venues. First, it can, in most cases, quite easily dedicate appropriate sites for the conference business: this assumption certainly holds if we are considering a modular approach in the planning of infrastructure. Second, an inside-the-airport venue may minimise travel times for delegates. This is a particularly strong advantage in the case of short or one-day meetings, where the impact, either from the economic or timing aspect, of transfer to downtown sites is much more significant. Thus, the development of a package of conference services within terminal walls provides a chance for an airport to create, close to the traditional hub concept of the airline business, a role of conference and meeting centre, or a conference hub. This is the case, for instance, in Charles De Gaulle airport in Paris, which today is a world best-in-class performer for airport conference services. Here the implementation of this kind of ancillary service has permitted the airport to strengthen its competitive position on the market well beyond the marketing performance of the hub carrier Air France. Another good example is provided by London City Airport, where meeting facilities have been welcomed by the business communities, with record load factors for these ancillary infrastructures.

Developing congressional facilities can be implemented by means of three different approaches:

- *in-terminal facilities directly managed by the airport enterprise itself.* This technique is implemented when airports aim to improve their own direct market awareness: in this case, launching a new innovative service, like this one, may become a distinctive feature for a site. However, this approach may also lead to significant economic and financial risks. In fact, the direct management of operational costs, most of them fixed, by the airport raises dramatically the break-even point for this activity. Some practices are now under evaluation in various European sites, basically as an expansion of the concept of airline lounges or as a way to convert abandoned or underused areas of terminal buildings;

- *in-terminal facilities outsourced* and then managed by a concessionaire. This is usually the first choice for airports, as economic risk is transferred to a third party. Its specific expertise will be helpful in terms of improving both the business's return on investment and the magnitude of royalties for the airport enterprise. This is what happens, for instance, at Geneva, London City or Rome, where dedicated professional outsourcers manage this business;
- *partnership with hotel chain*, which can be implemented through the building of hotels within or close to airport boundaries. This formula significantly stretches the value proposition and usually targets larger-scale or long-term meetings, with a chance to rest at the hotel overnight. This approach is followed by Paris CDG, London Heathrow and Gatwick and by many US airports.

Logistics Services and Property Management

Historically, airports have played a modest role as partners to their related industries. In other words, the airport infrastructure has not been deeply integrated in firms' logistic chains, but simply used as an 'external' medium as well as transfer point for goods, with a role of facilitating material contacts between the spokes of the chain itself.

Today, however, on the basis of significant experiences, mainly in the maritime industry,[6] even airport enterprises are starting to develop an enriched cargo portfolio offer for firms in their own catchment area. For instance, operations such as the partial transformation of products or semi-components may help to increase the average load factors for the airport's cargo city, while offering the whole industrial sector new and lower-cost alternatives to the traditional proprietary warehouse approach.

Another possibility is lending spare space in airport cargo facilities to host fairs and exhibitions, especially technical ones. In this case, a magnitude of synergies can be exploited with both the conference business, and also hotel chains.

The airport enterprise, however, can also promote the renting of all spaces – either built or planned – that are located within its own boundaries. This activity is referred to as property management and looks at companies with a significant visibility on international markets, such as multinationals, as a primary target. For these companies, establishing their

---

[6] As in the case of Rotterdam port area with the establishment of Distriparks.

headquarters or a national subsidiary close to or within an airport may turn out to become a critical factor of success in terms of cutting logistic and personnel costs. This formula has been widely implemented in the case of Amsterdam and Vienna airports.

> *Amsterdam Airport Authority has created a subsidiary, named Schiphol Real Estate, which is responsible for development projects, investment and building of new sites within the airport site together with some specific partners. Another area of business comes from the renting of land and buildings to various subjects, most of them multinationals, like Unilever, for instance. Another good example comes from Portland in the US. Here the airport authority has awarded Bechtel the rights for the exploitation of 120 acres and the building of a light railway to connect this area to downtown. In this site a number of different facilities, like post offices, business and shopping centres will be hosted.*

Opportunities for sound economic exploitations of the property management business also exist in the case of regional airports. In this case the primary target will be, for instance, consulting firms or other kinds of companies that need only a temporary location in the area. In this case, however, airports will have to face stiffer competition from both companies who specialise in temporary rents, as well as from hotels.

Consulting Services

Best-in-class airport operators may, eventually, implement another form of upgrade of their service package offered to the market. They can, for instance, assist and support both new-comers in the airport business and existing players when opening new infrastructures or expanding old ones. Here, their role consists of the selling of their practical expertise with the aim to improve other actors' skills through the transfer of the latest managerial know-how and competencies. On the one hand, the consulting approach is consistent with the technical activities of project engineering and financial management: for instance, SEA, the airport authority responsible for the Milan area airports, has recently supported the expansion plan of Bucarest/Otopeni airport and is now supervising the restoration works for Sarajevo airport.

On the other hand, the consulting activity will mainly deal with the implementation of management contracts. In this case, the most innovative component of the 'commercial airport' format will be exported.

A Best-in-Class Airport Enterprise: BAA and the Non-Aviation Business

BAA is perhaps the world's leading airport operator in terms of traffic volume and innovation, particularly in the development of retailing. It operates 7 airports in the UK and it is active also in the USA (Pittsburgh, Indianapolis being some notable examples) and in Australia.

BAA's non-aviation philosophy is 'to put customers first and concentrate on their needs'. The company aims to create what it terms a 'total retail environment', the key components of this strategy including:

- positive competition;
- branded operations and wide product ranges;
- fair pricing;
- guaranteed value for money;
- high service levels;
- continuous improvement and innovation.

BAA continuously maps customer satisfaction by means of technical tools, such as QSM. The QSM is a detailed survey of passengers, covering service standards and value for money. It is designed to track the airports' overall performance and to highlight areas of weakness. Improvement and innovation are also helped by the structure of the airports' retail departments – they are organised by function, with specialist product managers running individual retail sectors (Humphries, 1996). Specific examples of innovations include:

- retailing management contracts in which BAA pays a management fee to the retailers and retains all sales turnovers as revenue. Such contracts enable a longer-term view by both BAA and concessionaires;[7]
- Bonus Points frequency-shopping card;[8]
- a personal shopping service at Heathrow's Terminal 4, just one example of the levels of service provided at BAA airports;

---

[7] The rate of innovation of this formula lies in the fact that the management contract approach is actually applied in the reverse form than the usual one described at charter 4.

[8] The subject concerning frequency-shopping cards and loyalty schemes will be explored in more depth in the next chapter.

- a 'theme park' at Gatwick, named 'Gatwick and Aviation, Past, Present and Future'. The idea for a Gatwick attraction arose from the fact that the airport is already among the top five fee-paying attractions in the south-east of England. The park is usually busy in the late morning to mid-afternoon period, when the airport is most lightly used.

'Best Airport in the World': The Case of Singapore Airport

Singapore is an excellent example of a quasi-city state with virtually no origin & destination (O&D) demand that has been able to acquire over the years a solid role for stopover traffic between Europe and Australia, along the so-called 'Kangaroo Route'. Singapore Airlines is consistently considered the best airline in the world and the pace of passengers that are choosing Singapore as a stopover for their Asian flights has been constantly increasing for the last decade.

Singapore airport is famous throughout the world for its own unconventional and rather innovative package. Travellers may pass their time before boarding not only shopping in the various arcades of the complex, but also relaxing close to an artificial lake surrounded by orchids. Between a long list of bars and pubs, it's also possible to have a drink while listening to a violinist within an environment of tropical palms and reproductions of past civil airliners. Children may play their favourite videogame in a dedicated area, while film lovers will find a movie theatre and sport fans a sports arena. There is also a fitness centre close to the Transit Hotel at Terminal 1, where you can also have a sauna or Jacuzzi.

For aviation enthusiasts there is a garden terrace with chairs, tables, umbrellas and an excellent view of the runway and no limits for shooting pictures. And when transit passengers have to wait for five hours before the next flight is going to depart, they have the chance of taking a free city tour including a boat trip on the river.

In 2000 Changi airport was awarded by IATA 'Best Airport Worldwide' in the category of more than 25 million passengers per year. More than 60% of the annual revenues of the airport comes from the non-aviation related business.

Chapter 6

Achieving Sustainable Growth for the 'Commercial Airport' Concept: The Role of Loyalty Schemes

The Role and Meaning of Loyalty for a Service Company

A firm's value, in whatever kind of industry, poses its primary pillars on its own customer portfolio's strength (Lovelock, 1984; Kotler and Scott, 1997).

In other words, core dimensions of a company's success are today related not only to absolute numbers of yearly market transactions, but also to the level of loyal customers that a company is able to achieve and then manage over time (Berry, 1986). On the one hand, overall quantitative figures concerning provider-customer interactions may be significant but also misleading, as they can show variance even over a short amount of time (like one year) according to macro and micro erratic changes. On the other hand, a solid loyal base[1] will assure a consistent path of growth for a company and reinforce the achievement of a long-term market competitive advantage (Hamel, 2000). Loyal customers will typically act not only as repetitive purchasers of the same brand, but also as company advocates through the diffusion of positive 'word-of-mouth' among their peers. Loyalty, thus, may be considered a key indicator of a company's market success, as it leads to increasing revenues, collapsing marketing costs[2] and hopefully, rocketing profits.

---

[1] For instance, the so-called 'Pareto rule' states that in all industries, 80% of a company's revenues come from 20% of its best customers, also named key accounts. As a consequence, companies have to adopt some 'key account management' activities to retain their best customers. This places the role of loyalty at the core of a best-in-class company's customer focus.

[2] A loyal customer will be typically reached through direct marketing communications that are far more efficient than generic advertising. A direct communication, in the form of e-mails for instance, will cost less to a company whilst improving a message's effectiveness to the customer, frequently by means of high personalisation.

To improve customers' loyalty a firm must first identify them, then systematically trace their purchase behaviour and finally transform gathered data into knowledge to provide an effective marketing action for that target. This is particularly important in the case of a service company, where the value proposition's intangibility[3] means that customers frequently have no chance to test it before purchase and consumption (Levitt, 1980 and 1999; Lovelock, 1984). In this case, thus, loyalty and word-of-mouth become a company's best intangible assets and a key to achieving market dominance.

One of the most successful tools used to achieve these goals involves the introduction of fidelity schemes, or loyalty cards, in many B2C service contexts. Loyalty cards are the most tangible evidence of what many practitioners call 'marketing information revolution'. The most sought-after result of loyalty cards lies in the acquisition of increasing shares of customers' time and money, both of which are valid indicators of loyalty itself. Loyal targets are then typically offered some rewards that tend to increase as their loyalty improves over time. In other words, firms are willing to pay back customers for what they are gaining in terms of superior knowledge of purchase patterns.

Nevertheless, there are many cases in which loyalty cards have shown disappointing performances when compared to management's expectations. For example, Safeway, a UK retailer brand, withdrew in 2000 its ABC Card after having collected around 10 million cards. Reasons for failure can differ. Scarce use of data, due to lack of time and technical knowledge to process it; errors in data gathering processes; and, eventually, a similarity between competitors' loyalty schemes, may push customers to cherry pick and benefit from seasonal promotional offers. In a broader sense, however, loyalty programs, although complex and costly tools, are today becoming key drivers to consolidate provider-customer relationships. Moreover, they represent a core pillar of much more comprehensive Customer Relationship Management (CRM) approaches. In the microenvironment of services, the use of fidelity schemes to improve long-term market relationships was first seen in the airline business, where many carriers have been using them since the early 1980s (Hanlon,. 1986; Doganis, 2001).

---

[3] On the contrary, customers are able to test products before purchasing. Their direct empirical evidence, thus, drives consumption choices.

Benchmarking Airlines' Experience

Between the late 1970s and early 1980s, airline deregulation in the US market lifted both capacity and price caps. This new environment resulted in a huge number of start-ups entering the market, some of them having a highly aggressive tariff proposition, as in the case of low-cost carriers (Morrison and Winston, 1995).

In the early periods, a price-war forced incumbents to react and match new comers' low fares as a short-term tactic to protect their volume market shares. Later, however, this strategic choice resulted in a number of financially unsustainable positions and to some incumbents' bankruptcies, as in the case of Braniff. As a consequence of this, trunk carriers faced a need to return to some form of non-price competition and create differentiation, in an era of growing commoditisation, by acting on the value proposition's service side.

Loyalty rewarding schemes, in the form of the so-called Frequent-Flyer Programs (FFPs), proved to be the most dramatic innovation in this changing market scenario. Thanks to the implementation of a FFP, an airline was given the chance to acquire new forms of competitive advantage, which was maximised in the case of the pioneer-carrier that first introduced this marketing shake-out. It was American Airlines, back in 1981, who launched the first frequent flyer program (FFP), naming it AAdvantage. At the dawn of US airline deregulation, the Dallas-based carrier was keen to realise the strategic importance of learning more about the travel patterns of its best customers, which were typically granted with air miles and free travel on the basis of the number of flights taken. At the beginning, this innovative tool proved to be very successful for American Airlines both in retaining its own customers and in responding to low-cost carriers' threats. However, it was shortly imitated by all other industry players, both mega carriers with dedicated programs, and regionals, by becoming partners of major carriers' schemes.

FFPs, more specifically, have provided a solution to a number of significant supplier-customer issues. The first one deals with the fact that, in highly competitive environments, a new customer's acquisition cost is up to five times more compared to a monopolistic regime (D'Aveni, 1994). This proves that customer equity is strictly correlated with the time duration of the commercial relationship, or Customer Life Time Value (CLTV). In this sense, FFPs have provided a positive stimulation to both actual and future return on investments, thanks to their combined action not only on the frequency of purchases, but also on the quality of market transactions, as loyal customers tend to become rather price inelastic.

Another topic of interest for FFPs is related to the level of analytical customer profiling they may generate, thanks to a huge and extraordinary quantity of detailed information about personal data, travel patterns,[4] plus ancillary expenses when using a FFP's partner. The huge interest born after the introduction of FFPs in the airline market, in fact, would lead other industries' providers to piggy back on an existing scheme, with financial institutions, credit card operators, telecommunication providers, hotel chains, car rentals, publishing companies, and grocery retailers being the most proactive ones.

For most, if not all, the affiliation with a FFP was actually a first step to address the rather new issue of customer retention, as their own industries were being faced with increased competitive pressure due to a move away from former monopolistic or sheltered market conditions. Although certainly costly tools, due to the choice to give away for free a service that would otherwise be tradable on the market and also the inherent handling costs, a number of these affiliated businesses decided to go on a stand-alone basis and replicate airlines' experience by establishing their own fidelity schemes. This decision was justified by the desire to increase per-capita expenditure and collect proprietary data about customers' purchase decisions and brand choices.

In any case, these actors seldom abandoned the established partnership with airlines that sometimes evolved into forms of close joint marketing actions. Indeed, many market operators, like retailer chains, introduced frequency-shopping cards, where more purchases meant more rapid rewards for the customer.

> One of the main examples in this case is provided by American Express. The credit card giant, after a 'below-the line' initial partnership with many airline FFPs, developed its own loyalty scheme, dubbed 'Membership Rewards'. This program works in the same form of a FFP by granting customers points according to the amount of purchases made with their Amex. When the customer reaches a certain level of reward, he/she may choose between huge portfolios of offers, with the core however formed by free tickets on many international airlines.

At the beginning of the 1990s, however, once their pioneer advantage had been lost due to competitors' imitation, some airlines started to work harder and develop new advanced tools for actively managing customer loyalty. Thus, some visionary carriers added to the basic frequency-shopping formula a stronger provider-customer interaction

---

[4] Both in terms of quantity (number of tickets) and quality (class of service purchased).

through phone calls, direct mailing, e-mail marketing and WAP interfaces. The goal was to shift from simply 'frequency-shopping' to a much more comprehensive 'customer loyalty' management. Here the strategic aim was, thus, to gain a continued feedback from the current customer portfolio and, thus, be able to work rapidly and promptly to adapt the offer system to the continually changing perceived priorities of the market.

The Provider-Customer Relational Link: The Case of Airport Enterprises

For airport entities, airlines were seen as the primary customer and as such meeting their needs satisfactorily was the primary goal. Satisfying the needs of tour operators, catering arms, General Sales Agents and travel agents was of secondary importance. End customers' satisfaction was not mapped nor was it considered a remarkable issue and, thus, almost never put on the agenda.

This broad underestimation of the customer's strategic role can be related to the substantial delay in market-oriented competences in the airport industry both in absolute terms and when compared to other service industries exposed to massive competition drivers. The lack of threats from the market simply meant there was no need to modify the *status quo* condition.

At this stage, it was not good news for airport managers to start their own marketing activity on the loyalty field having overlapping areas with airlines' loyalty-based strategic patterns. As airlines represented the first counterpart of airports in the value chain, strengthening B2B links was for airports a much more useful strategy to reach their final goal of increasing annual aircraft and passenger/cargo movements.

Given this mental approach, it would have been neither easy nor cheap to start B2C relationships in the absence of internal commitment, marketing-oriented core competences and budget-specific allocation. Moreover, airport managers decided not to start any promotional campaigns, aimed at attracting additional citizens inside the terminal, to avoid any interference with the classical logistical mission of maximising the efficiency of boarding and deboarding procedures. Mixing physical movements of passengers with non-passenger customers within the airport walls presented a risk for them in terms of creating confusion and leading to complaints from airlines for delay generation.

Consistent with this viewpoint, the only sort of tentative measure taken by airports to establish a relationship with a very limited number of passengers was in the form of so-called 'airport VIP cards'.

These cards[5] were typically granted for free to opinion-leader categories, like politicians or journalists.[6] These groups were offered, first of all, the privilege of being part of the restricted elite and, secondly, the benefit of a number of ancillary services, like accelerated check-in procedures, lounge access and dedicated assistance in case of flight cancellation, strikes or stand-by list. Unfortunately for airports, the same services were being offered by airlines to their top-tier frequent flyers, too. Thus, VIP cards never gained a distinctive visibility, particularly as this service was free of charge for some people and did not require any minimum annual miles flown like in the case of airlines' top tier levels.

However, by introducing a dramatic change from this past scenario the 'commercial airport' philosophy has totally reengineered the airport's selling process, which now requires an active managerial and marketing-driven approach, both in the phases of contact and attraction of potential customers and in the retention and fidelity of current ones.

In fact, the 'commercial airport' concept calls for the airport to act in exactly the same way as large department stores, assuming a role of 'network manager' in the relationship with the customer audience for all the terminal's commercial value propositions.

At this stage, even for airports it may become essential to develop and initiate some form of dedicated loyalty scheme, in the form of a so-called Airport Loyalty Program, or ALP.

Benefits from ALPs

For the commercial airport, thus, implementing an ALP could provide the opportunity to realise three kinds of benefits:

Increasing Royalties from Retailing Activities

Awarding customers with points or miles on the basis of each purchase within the terminal wall, from shopping venues to lounge access, or car rental services to hotel points, may be a major chance to increase per-capita purchases.

---

[5] Some of these programs are still working today.
[6] Other customer groups, instead, were paying huge fees for the same service to be granted.

As almost all retailing activities are operated on an outsourced basis, an airport enterprise will be able to realize an economic benefit from the improved commercial traffic in terms of the absolute magnitude of indirect revenues at the end of the fiscal year. Moreover, a substantial increase in a terminal's traffic figures will also enable the airport enterprise to renegotiate royalties paid by concessionaires. Some airports, for instance, could decide to link the size of each royalty with yearly passenger movements, this situation reinforcing, once again, the existing correlation between aviation and non-aviation related businesses.

Eventually, higher commercial figures in terms of passenger and customer movements[7] will create a chance to reengineer the whole retailing mix and attract top brand names. These top brands usually decide to operate only in situations of established patterns of demand and, thus, will be looking favourably at traffic data generated by the ALP within a commercial airport context. They will also be willing to pay higher royalties to the airport enterprise, too, if the previous condition takes place.

For this positive economic turnaround to apply, however, two strategic ingredients must be compulsory in an ALP formula.

First, an ALP should offer its own enrolled audience the chance to both collect and redeem points/miles in virtually every 'point of shopping', no exceptions being accepted by customers. Previous experience from BAA's Bonus Point frequency-shopping card, for instance, rewarded customers with a fixed catalogue of gifts, not necessarily correlated with the travel experience. Our suggestion, instead, provides for more complexities in its implementation as it needs full cooperation and commitment by all concessionaires, who typically act on a stand-alone and conflicting basis. The key to success is that the airport and all concessionaires should be seen not as landlord and tenants but as partners working together to improve their overall common business platform. This given, BAA's decision looked simpler to implement and to manage.

Second, an ALP needs to be structured in different levels exactly as in the case of airlines. This choice permits a segmentation of customers on the basis of their pattern of purchases (light, medium or heavy) and can prove to be very helpful for some dedicated promotional campaigns. The creation of different ALP levels may push on a customer's desire to reach the next superior level and status of awards. This condition, once again, may have a positive correlation with expenditure patterns at the terminal. The economic maximisation of customers' aspirations for the airport may be obtained when the status of benefit is granted not only on the basis of the

---

[7] The difference between passenger and customer movements has already been explored in Chapter 5.

quantity, but also the quality of purchases. Figure 6.1 shows a possible implementation of a three-tier level of ALP.

Increasing a Value Proposition's Effectiveness through Customer-Provider Interface.

As previously mentioned, the suggested form of ALP should look quite similar to the most advanced loyalty management practices acting in the market. Thus, a standard frequency-shopping template should be upgraded by associating it with deeper and constant information fluxes between airport and its customer database. Through standard tools, like newsletters and house-organs, for instance, or through technological-driven features like e-mails, the airport must create a bonding interface with its loyal target audience.

Figure 6.1   A possible three-tier ALP implementation

Level	Value offer	Targets
Standard	House-organ, newsletter, sales promotion.	Entry level for all customers joining the ALP.
Intermediate	Above services + airport ancillary services (i.e., 5 free entries to airport lounge).	Customers with intermediate purchase patterns.
Top	Above services + unlimited access to some airport ancillary services + large discounts at parking.	Customers with heavy purchase patterns who purchase value-added services (car rentals,info points, ticketing).

One of the main justifications for an ALP is based on the belief that a focused and tailored communication mix impacts on customers' behavioural patterns, and, as a consequence, may provoke new shopping visits in the terminal. In this case, an airport enterprise will assume a role of 'one-stop shopping' provider of an overall emotional experience for the customer.

The second one, asks for an airport enterprise to apply a deeper 'customer-centred' reengineering approach. This means, for instance that an airport's expansion plans will no longer be guided only by technical-based decisions that have lead to numerous misleading master plans. On the contrary, a marketing-driven philosophy will drive airport managers as a primary knowledge source in their long-term planning activities. Customers' feedback, obtained through an ALP, will provide these significant elements. A broader concept testing activity will be also encouraged due to a simpler identification of sample groups.

Moreover, a 'customer-centred' approach may be able to cut many costs related to a value proposition's innovation. With highly simplified concept testing , there will be a significant decrease in both the number of tested concepts and in the time frame involved in each concept.[8] This will enable the airport to get a more rapid payoff for its investments and, consequently, generate a positive impact on the company's share value and financial performance.

Reinforcing the Power of Attractiveness of an Airport's 'Commercial Catchment Area'

In a time of fierce competition between airports in aviation-related activities, an airport enterprise may choose to diversify its scope of activity by focusing on the enlargement of its 'commercial catchment area'. The size of an airport's commercial catchment area will grow in parallel with the increase and innovation of its non-aviation activities on a broader scale.

Obviously, when an airport enterprise chooses to apply this concept, new forms of inter-industry competition have to be taken into account: like in the case of neighbouring retailers, supermarkets, cinemas, discothèques, depending on the kind of product mix chosen.

In this unstable environment, the launch of an ALP becomes absolutely imperative if the airport management wants to attract and then retain new customers. In fact, it's fair to say that most of the new competitors in the airport industry have already launched some sort of frequency marketing tool.

---

[8] This time refers to the overall time period from the first concept presentation to its evaluation and modification.

Thus, if the airport enterprise wants to beat competitors, it will have to create a sort of new loyalty-generating product, in terms of the elements mentioned above at point 1.

The possible final outcome of such a strategy may be in the actual creation of different catchment areas, one related to the aviation business and under threat of narrowing, and the other, linked to the non-aviation business in a broad sense, able to significantly and continuously increase its own dimensions and market power.

Implementation of ALPs

It appears evident that the implementation of any form of loyalty scheme within the 'commercial airport' framework may turn into a major source of differentiation and reinforcement of the strategic position of airport management.

Nowadays, however, the trend towards a shift of strategic attention from aviation to non-aviation activities is not matched by an equal development of loyalty initiatives by airport enterprises.

In fact, there are really few examples concerning the implementation of both frequency shopping cards and loyalty schemes in the airport business. For instance, two examples can be found in the experience of BAA and of Bahrain International Airport.

In many cases, however, airports have found a simpler way through agreements with airlines by granting terminal customer FFP miles on the basis of the amount of purchases made, as in the case, for instance, of Italy's Aeroporti di Roma (ADR) with Alitalia's Millemiglia. This approach, as it is obviously cheaper and has shorter returns on investment, shows an 'ancien-regime' passive attitude of airports, leaving to airlines the role of leader in the provider-end customer relationship and also the ownership of all sensible customer information.

In this sense, if airports aim to really control final demand, they will have to initiate some major forms of dual interface with the end target by developing their own proprietary B2C interfaces. In this case, the ALP solution promises to be the best in terms of improving customer portfolio and, thus, revenue growth, as it has happened in other industries of the wider service environment.

Chapter 7

How to Construct an Airport Marketing Plan

A Creative Marketing Approach for the Airport Enterprise

Turbulent competitive dynamics in the airport business are forcing all players to reengineer their strategies as the only way to maintain long-term viability. Start-up of greenfield airports or the conversion of former military ones; deregulation processes in former monopoly 'cash-cows', like ground handling; growing competitive pressures from the likes of high-speed trains as well as videoconferencing; all of these combined elements mean that today market-based ingenuity has become crucial for airport enterprises. The adoption of a 'customer-centred' approach is capable of creating more satisfied customers which may be considered an effective basis to counteract both intra-industry and inter-value chain attacks.

This, however, does not mean that airports on a widespread basis are actually adopting a full-scale, marketing-based approach to manage their intermediate and final relationships. Most of the time, in fact, airports remain passive in both negotiations and market interactions with their target audiences, this position being a direct consequence of the historic lack of managerial know-how. What airports need today, is a cultural change in management practices, to move airport managers away from the pure exploitation of natural-monopoly rents towards a proactive view able to construct a solid competitive advantage in a turbulent scenario.

One of the main pillars of this new approach lies naturally in the planning of all strategic and operational duties to be implemented. Dealing specifically with marketing, the definition of an airport marketing plan is a fundamental step for establishing new 'rules of conduct' and later implementing them in a consistent way.

We may define the contents of an airport marketing plan into four phases:

- An assessment of the firm's macro and micro competitive position;

- a definition of the main goals and objectives for the airport enterprise;
- implementation of the chosen objectives;
- auditing of actual performances achieved.

Assessment

A first goal of the diagnosis phase lies in the analytical evaluation of each product-market combination in which the airport enterprise operates. Moreover, it also aims to map the nature and intensity of current relationships with intermediate and final customers. On completion, this phase should provide a good picture of the airport's past and current competitive position. Understanding macro and micro boundaries should help managers to adopt a consistent package of operational decisions and improve the airport's position by removing weakness, while reinforcing existing key success factors.

The assesment can be split into two different viewpoints:

- how did the airport's market position change since the last period of observation?[1]
- what is the airport's current market position?

Main Drivers of Change Which have Occurred in Recent Years

Here the main aspects to be considered refer to macro environmental changes that have impacted on the business performance during the time period in question. For instance, we may think of the SARS epidemic or the post-September 11 environment, or the Iraqi and Afghanistan wars, not to mention Euro-dollar exchange rate fluctuations and OPEC's decisions about oil production levels. Figure 7.1 sums up the main possible drivers of macro environmental change.

Managers have to check if all past economic and commercial goals have actually been achieved. Some key performance indexes (KPIs) that should be taken into consideration refer, for instance, to the amount of forecasted passengers or to the percentage of connecting passengers, if we are referring to a primary hub airport.

This kind of analysis, which should be conducted on a broader scale to include all strategic business units (SBUs), must involve financial

---

[1] A good tactic is to consider performance in the last six months.

figures, too. In this case, each SBU's ROI must be compared with internal past figures (internal benchmarking) or by matching airport data with both best-in-class intra-industry performers and with zero-risk financial activities, like State bonds (external benchmarking).[2]

Figure 7.1 The main types of macro environmental changes concerning the airport industry

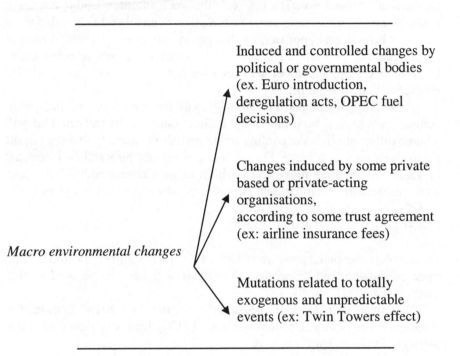

Macro environmental changes

Induced and controlled changes by political or governmental bodies (ex. Euro introduction, deregulation acts, OPEC fuel decisions)

Changes induced by some private based or private-acting organisations, according to some trust agreement (ex: airline insurance fees)

Mutations related to totally exogenous and unpredictable events (ex: Twin Towers effect)

One of the main problems concerning external benchmarking lies in how to gather this critical information. Industry associations could be an initial source, even if this data is usually old and manipulated. Some other field tactics, like the 'mystery shopper' approach[3], could follow. Finally, alliances may provide a good platform for data exchange between partners.

---

[2] This kind of analysis will be aimed firstly at identifying a risk premium for the airport business. Usually this value is expressed as a percentage that has to be added to that of the zero-risk bond for comparison.
[3] This field tactic requires the use of dedicated professionals to collect data by direct observation on the field and P&L analysis of key competitors.

Later on, a portfolio analysis will be conducted on the overall airport's B2B and B2C relationships. This tool will evaluate the quality levels of market links by measuring loyalty achieved on intermediate and final customers, the latter one being possible only in the case of an existing Airport Loyalty Program (ALP).

Moreover, in the case of B2B transactions, airport managers will have to fully understand the reasons behind any kind of market transaction's breakdown. The reason is that such an unfavourable condition could be due to some exogenous factors, like September 11, but also to an incorrect behavioural approach by the airport enterprise. A detailed map of these situations of ineffectiveness will be crucial not only to drive short-term[4] recovery strategies but also improve managerial skills and portfolio efficiency in the long term.

Finally, a competitive analysis will be considered to fully map competitors' moves, both direct and indirect ones, in the market. This will assume different scopes according to the market positioning that the airport enterprise wants to achieve. For instance, a primary hub will be interested in tracing competitive moves only within its own cluster and will not take into consideration what regional airports have done over the last year.

The Airport's Current Market Condition

To complete the picture we must look at the firm's current position. The same aforementioned categories of analysis will have to be used in this case.

A typical tool used to illustrate an airport's current competitive situation is the Boston Consulting Group (BCG) matrix designed for each Strategic Business Unit involved.

Definition of Goals

This second phase asks airport managers to explore, and later adopt, one of the main available strategic marketing options, like:

- the 'fight option', that promises to increase an airport's market share;

---

[4] This tool refers to the bundle of operational actions that a company may put into action to manage a dissatisfied customer and possibly stimulate him to return to a situation of active purchaser.

- The 'retrench option', that works to protect the current market share in a highly turbulent environment;
- The 'streamlining option', that looks at divesting unprofitable SBUs;
- The 'abandon option', that sees a company exiting a current business.

Fighting for Acquiring New Market Power

This is always the preferred option by both airport managers and political stakeholders, as it is linked to positive and rather successful policies. This option seems, however, to require a high level of stability in both macro and micro scenario drivers. In fact, an airport's market growth is due not only to successful internal KPIs, but also to both a growing primary demand and a stable competitive environment as well.

An airport management may define this goal through a bundle of operational activities:

- by fostering the effectiveness of actual market relationships with served customers. Improving their loyalty indexes will provide a good chance to make these players concentrate a larger slice of their activity on a single airport platform;
- by maximising the quality of business development processes through the use of dedicated intelligence and IT supports. This could be the result of an excellent aviation-related marketing campaign, where the airport succeeds in attracting new airlines thanks to the scope of its value proposition in terms of information and marketing support packages;
- by diversifying the range of services offered and targeting both current and potential customers. In the case of current customers, providing extra retailing corners in the terminal building will be a good trick to improve both customer satisfaction and the length of time spent in the terminal building, with an associated effect on the average expenditure level. In the case of potential customers, a more radical innovation in the non-aviation activity, like the launch of discothèques and supermarkets, will attract new non-passenger cluster targets and extend the power of commercial influence.

Figure 7.2 draws these four tactics together by placing them in the famous Ansoff matrix.

Figure 7.2 Four strategies to improve market shares in the airport business

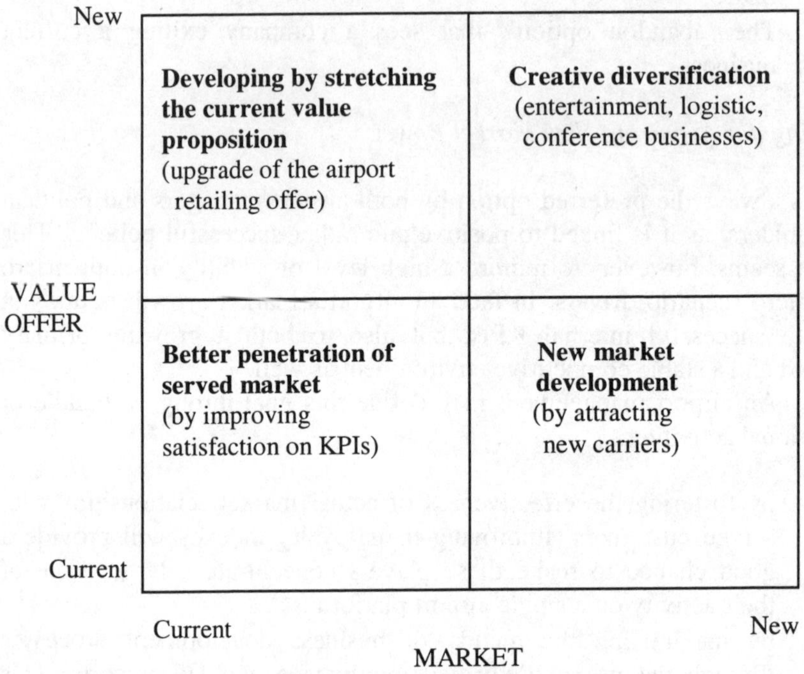

	Current ← MARKET → **New**	
New ↑ VALUE OFFER ↓ **Current**	**Developing by stretching the current value proposition** (upgrade of the airport retailing offer)	**Creative diversification** (entertainment, logistic, conference businesses)
	Better penetration of served market (by improving satisfaction on KPIs)	**New market development** (by attracting new carriers)

Reinforcing and Defending Current Market Share

Hypercompetition and stagnation in demand levels, as a consequence of economic recession, requires airports to focus on a less aggressive and more conservative strategy.

This option suggests that airport managers identify similar target goals to those of the previous year. Thus, in a hyper-turbulent environment, maintaining the current financial and competitive position should be considered a significant success.

The retrench tactic will permit the airport to act and focus on its core competencies and, thus, reinforce its drivers of competitive advantage. At the end of the downturn, the players who survive would be able to turn once again to a growth strategy.

Divesting

A negative economic climate may require airports to take much more drastic decisions. One of these is the need to cut unprofitable business units as a means to rationalise the portfolio of offer and improve overall efficiency.

This activity is frequently implemented by giving away a slice of the current business to a third party concessionaire. In the case of aviation-related activities, this could involve the practice of outsourcing handling services and dismantling the internal production, while conserving the marketing-related activities concerning scouting for new carriers.

In the non-aviation business, airport managers could instead decide to give away to a third-party specialised concessionaire the management of properties to improve the market performance that may be gained from this business.

> *In the case of airlines, divesting is common in the case of frequency reductions on a certain route or eventually to an entire route cut. Airlines typically act like this to reduce their burden of losses, even if the carrier's overall visibility is also negatively impacted in terms of being less attractive for passengers, especially business ones.*

Abandon an Entire SBU

This option is the most painful one for any company as it causes severe socio-economic consequences, like job redundancies and possible interference by political actors.

It tends to be cautiously used in the airport business and may deal with the non-aviation business only, as aviation-business practices remain the technical core of the airport enterprise.

In the case of non-aviation related businesses, this decision could be represented by a management contract, in which all terminal activities are given to a concessionaire that will pay some royalties or fixed income to the landlord.

Clearly, an airport management will have to choose between one of these four paths and then implement it on a consistent basis.

Implementation of Objectives

This phase will typically deal with:

- timing of activities to be followed and achieve desired goals;
- assignment of responsibilities;
- definition of the budget of economic resources.

Timing of Activities

This operational practice aims to define a schedule for all operations that will be taken and achieve the desired results. On the one hand, this kind of timetable will be correlated to a number of endogenous constraints, like:

- infrastructural constraints, that could pose a limit to a projected upgrade of retailing facilities, requiring, for instance, an extension of terminal spaces to firstly be implemented;
- organisational constraints, referring to a lack of flexibility in job positions, leading to longer execution and response-to-market times;
- financial constraints, related to negative cash-flows that would necessitate borrowing money on the market with inherent delays in operating procedures.

On the other hand, timing decisions will be correlated with exogenous factors, like aggressive moves by competitors. This will clearly force an airport enterprise to compress its timing steps so as not to lose market share and frequently to borrow extra capacity on the market, especially labour capacity, on a short-time basis.

A quieter environment will instead mean that airport managers can structure their schedule of activities more accordingly with endogenous constraints.

Assignment of Responsibilities

This phase seems consistent with a 'management by objectives' logic of conduct. In this case, a project manager is identified and he/she will become responsible for all coordination duties of the group of peers and provide stakeholders with the expected sound economic results as well.

Some best-in-class airport companies are already abandoning a strict functional organisation and adopting more complex divisional and mixed solutions that take into account the tool of project managing.

Budgeting

Assigning the correct amount of resources seems a crucial step on the path to reach some sort of company goal.

For instance, a limited budget could force managers to use only second-best tools in communicating their value proposition to the market. Over-budgeting might instead create some internal 'islands of ineffectiveness', with employees proving to be less committed in reaching challenging results and, therefore, leading to chronic weaknesses.

Auditing of Financial Results

The fourth and last part of the airport marketing plan deals with performance auditing. It maintains some distinctive elements, the first one related to its timing. This activity, in fact, logically follows on from the first three planning phases.

Nevertheless, the results of the auditing phase will be critically helpful in suggesting some milestones to be included in the next plan's diagnosis. This interdependence emphasises the circular, long-term view that links each marketing plan of the airport enterprise, as each covers a short-term perspective (usually 1-2 years) but is directly linked to the previous one.

The two subparts that compose the auditing phase are:

- gap analysis,
- definition of corrective hypotheses to smooth, in the next plan, the kind of gaps identified and targeted.

Gap Analysis

Here each SBU's actual and budget values and all airport's internal and external processes are identified.

Regarding competitive data, market share is the main parameter to be taken into account. A negative gap may be ascribed for a number of reasons. First, these difficulties may be due to a rapid and unforeseeable change in the 'rules of the game' of the industry: like in the case of the introduction of governmental decrees that limit the daily range of operations, or the attack by new competitors or, eventually, some random events.[5]

Nevertheless, a negative result could be explained by an error in the budget planning. This often occurs when managers choose to fix too many challenging goals, which cannot actually be achieved due to some organisation or structural weaknesses or because a competitors' role had been underestimated. A practice like this has to be kept under strict observation, because it can produce some negative behaviour in the mind of airport employees, when they perceive them as impossible to be reached.

Definition of Corrective Hypotheses

An airport management, on the basis of the figures described above, will have to define some corrective actions to be implemented in the next diagnosis.

This kind of qualitative contribution appears crucial because it forces managers to make a hierarchy of priorities by identifying the most relevant ones.

Some Concluding Remarks about Airport Marketing Planning

The bundle of changes that airports are now being faced with are too relevant and will certainly take them, at the end, to rather different industry boundaries than the existing ones.

This increasingly complex microenvironment tends to extend the scope of marketing planning and its implementation in both analytical and professional terms. In other words, the later an airport improves both managerial skills and knowledge capabilities, the higher will be the risk of market marginalisation and, thus, to be able to survive only in a niche perspective. No more protectionist barriers will be able to prevent this situation, either at a domestic or global scale.

The example of London City Airport, a private airport that has passed from 35,000[6] to more than 2 million passengers per annum in a rather short space of time, proves that passive conducts may be dangerous even in the case of first-tier performers. This kind of marketing lesson, however, should provide a positive stimulation as well for all new comers in the new Millennium's airport industry. Market-rents may not exist in

---

[5] Like wars or terrorist attacks.
[6] These data refer to 1987 figures.

hypercompetitive territories; only a purely reactive and fearful behaviour may justify them. But it's also true that to successfully win, airports have to deeply reengineer their value proposition according to the paradigms of a 'customer-centred view' and offer the target market an offer which is consistent with their expectations.

London City Airport: A Best-in-Class Provider in the Airport Business

London City Airport (LCA) was inaugurated in 1987. Nowadays, it probably represents the world's best-in-class example of a private airport enterprise.

Looking back to the early 1980s, the core of LCA's strategic design was the idea that a new infrastructure could become a primary catalyser for the outgoing and incoming business community in the Docks area.

There were however significant technical obstacles which had to be overcome before aircraft operations could commence on the new site. Firstly, available space for ground movements was scarce, as the taxiway was to be built on a strip of land reclaimed from the river Thames. This situation would provide a limit to the number of yearly slots that was initially fixed at 10 per hour. It was also impossible to build a parallel taxiway. Secondly, the limited runway length – only 800 meters! – would require airlines to operate small turboprop aircraft, like 50-seater Dash7s, this model being the only one to be fully compliant with a steep 7.5° approach instead of an usual 3° descent. Finally, air space congestion and nearby obstacles, like the Canary Wharf building, would impose, in any case, an upper slot cap of 12 per hour.

Based on these figures, LCA's inauguration actually introduced very limited additional capacity to the congested London area, with a small chance of becoming a head-to-head competitor with the much larger airports at Heathrow, Gatwick, Stansted and Luton. LCA, however, could exploit its favourable geographic location to attract high-yield O&D passengers flying between London and some main business centres.

Early economic and competitive results, when compared with an initial investment of 15 million pounds, were discouraging. In 1990, LCA reached only 200,000 passengers: difficulties in accessing the airport (no subways were available) and longer flying times, due to turboprop operations, were preventing a lot of potential customers from choosing LCA.

In 1991, however, LCA was able to attract 50% of English business traffic and 30% of foreign business traffic flying between London and Brussels, Paris and Rotterdam. 70% of these passengers were paying full fares, when compared with only 27% in the case of Heathrow. 1991 saw also the decision to extend the airport's runway length to 1199 meters. These improvements would mean an additional investment of 41 million pounds. This decision, however, would enable the landing and take-off of Bae146 regional jets at LCA. Bae146s also named 'whisper jets' were able to carry around 100 passengers on a much longer range than turboprops while significantly upgrading on-board comfort, too. In the same period, a new weekly slot cap was fixed at 130.

From that moment onwards LCA's story has been paved with many successful milestones. In 1995 the airport managed 550,000 passengers, while in 1997 this figure reached 1.16 million and in 2000 1.6 million passengers.

Today LCA is served by all the main European carriers, either directly or, more often, by their regional franchisees or associates. These airlines look for the opportunity to collect premium connecting volumes for their hubs, like Paris or Frankfurt, or focus on point-to-point traffics only, as it is the case of VLM, a Belgian carrier operating 7 times per day on the LCA-Rotterdam route.

LCA, which has since been sold by Mowlem, an engineering company, to an Irish entrepreneur, represents today a formidable competitor for BAA's Heathrow, Gatwick and Stansted. BAA was forced to establish a new high-speed connection between Heathrow and Paddington Station to counteract this threat and protect its share of high-yield passengers. LCA is also considered an icon of the 'city airport' concept, as its management was able to turn structural weaknesses into competitive points of strengths.

LCA's airport management approach may be broken down into four main pillars. The first one has been the creation of a permanent joint committee between the airport authority and citizens' representatives, with the goal of discussing both occasions of growth for the airport and the pace of negative externalities generated by aircraft operations. This kind of cooperative approach between the various airport shareholders has contributed to nearby residents accepting both the runway extension and a progressive increase in the number of weekly slots to reach the current level of 260.

Second, LCA has strictly cooperated with regional aircraft manufacturers to reach full operational ability and certification to land their various types of aircraft at LCA. We already mentioned the inauguration of Bae146 operations as a key element for the increase in passenger numbers, thanks to their superior capacity compared to turboprop models.

Third, LCA management has strongly believed in an airport-related marketing strategy aimed at extending the number of connections and attracting new operators to its airport. This activity has been implemented by using market research studies on a large scale and by formulating innovative value packages for prospect carriers.

Fourth, the terminal building has been designed to provide excellence in the most significant processes for its business target audience. The Minimum Check-in Time (MCT) now is ten minutes prior to flight departure. Baggage delivery times have also been compressed.

In April 2000 LCA management presented a new expansion plan, which, once realised, should allow the airport to manage 3.5 up to 4 million passengers per year with employees more than doubling from a current level of 1,300 to 2,800. A new remote aircraft parking site will be built and the existing apron will be extended, with an extra office building, a connecting taxiway, car park and a holding point for departing aircraft also to be added. This bundle of upgrades, with an estimated value of 20 million pounds, should all be completed within 2004, when the Dockland Light Railway, linking LCA and the Docks area with downtown London, should be operational, too.

Chapter 8

September 11 Attacks[1]

'Terrorists do have something in common with airlines after all: they both operate internationally'

(Rod Eddington, CEO, British Airways, speaking in Washington early 2004 at the end of an extraordinary few weeks of security alerts on the North Atlantic)

September 11, 2001 in New York and Washington

The tragic events of September 11, 2001 saw for the first time the use of civil aircraft as vectors of death on a large scale. These events, however, promoted a significant response by all bodies in charge of international aviation security issues.

On the one hand, the European Civil Aviation Conference,[2] for instance, decided to form a special interest group just a few days after the terrorist attacks took place. When they met for the first time in Bordeaux on September 20 and 21, 2001, they agreed to establish three task forces to examine all security issues and provide rational and sustainable measures to be applied. These task forces hosted officials from the US Federal Aviation Administration, Israeli and Japanese Civil Aviation Authorities and from the European Union.

At the same time, US bodies immediately introduced some prohibitions, many of them later abandoned. This insecure approach clearly showed a condition of modest knowledge and experience in the security area by American authorities. The reason for this situation lies in the fact that terrorism has been considered for a long time by the US as an exclusively European or Middle Eastern problem. This belief had prompted

---

[1] This chapter has been co-written with Alfredo Roma. Mr. Roma is the former Chairman of ENAC, the Italian Civil Aviation Authority, and President of the European Civil Aviation Conference (ECAC).

[2] ECAC is a pan European body with 41 members.

US airports to adopt quite limited security actions, a fact that had been apparent for many years to European travellers. Evidence of this is provided by the fact that before September 11, 2001 America inspected only 5% of checked baggage and used only 33 guards, known as sky marshals, to protect sensitive flights. In contrast, US carriers had already imposed tight security measures for their operations in European airports.

In a similar vein, on September 14, 2001 an *ad-hoc* EU Council created a multidisciplinary group, formed by experts in the areas of security, justice and internal affairs and by representatives of ICAO, ECAC, Eurocontrol and US Aviation Authorities to deal with coordination and cooperation practices in the security field within the Union's boundaries.

An Institutional Picture of Security Practices in the Airport Business

Concerning this topic, it is possible to look at two different categories of legal fronts.

On the one hand, there are the requirements fixed by ICAO and ECAC's DOC.30, which unfortunately relate only to international flights. On the other hand, all internal rules assumed by each individual country in the area of security may be considered. The latter are defined, from time to time, by local Internal Affairs, Justice or Defence Ministries, or by a combination of other technical bodies. This creates confusion and evidence of dispersion of ruling control between too many actors.

The ECAC's DOC.30 would have been able to guarantee a good level of security,[3] even if these measures were not enough to avoid September 11's terrorism attacks. The main problems arising from this document relate to:

- application, which, as already mentioned, works only on international flights;
- problems related with X-ray control for belly baggage, originally due to be in force since January 1, 2003, but still not fully operational in all contexts;
- mixture of both incoming and departing passengers in many European airports, as is the case in Rome Fiumicino and Frankfurt terminal buildings. In this case, an incoming passenger from an airport with

---

[3] If applied in the US domestic air market at the time of September 11 attacks.

lower security measures could easily get in contact with a departing one and create an element of risk;

- differences from one country to another in the field of financial resources and training of personnel involved in the security area.

Measures Proposed by the United States

On November 16, 2001 the US Administration ruled out the constitution of an Undersecretary for Security, hierarchically under the Department of Transportation, but separated from the Federal Aviation Administration (FAA). Moreover, new air security measures were also being included in the Aviation and Transportation Security Act, dealing with security discipline both on the ground and during flights.

In the case of cruising phases, a number of packages of implementation were decided. The first one imposed the locking of cockpit doors and their reinforcement. Another later suggestion was the installation of video cameras to give pilots a constant view of the main cabin; a protected transponder and new codes for ground/cockpit/ground communications. A massive use of sky marshals would be considered, too, on the basis of the decades-long experience provided by El-Al. Finally, the US have been asking for some European carriers operating in its own airspace to use sky marshals aboard their planes. Unfortunately, some of them have refused and have opposed this measure, preferring, in the case of sensitive intelligence information, to cancel flights.

> *Israeli's El Al has been using sky marshals for more than 30 years and they have foiled a number of hijacking attempts. Sky marshals are present on every El Al flight and their number can vary according to the type of aircraft flown and the destination served. They are all armed with automatic hand-guns, carried in quick-draw holsters. Their last known service dates back to November 17, 2002, when a hijack attempt on a flight from Tel Aviv to Istanbul was foiled. An attacker tried to break into the cockpit with a small folding knife, but the security guards subdued him in seconds.*

Security measures to be implemented on the ground included the reinforcement of airport boundaries by means of dedicated personnel; tight controls of those people accessing airports for job-related purposes; the testing of new biometric devices to identify passengers; the purchase of hundreds of new Explosive Detection System (EDS) machines for screening of all baggage; a specific training for flight personnel in the case of a terrorist event; and an upgraded surveillance of parking aircraft at night, including mail and cargo operators.

Now all one billion bags checked on to international flights in America each year are supposed to be inspected and tens of thousands of flights each month carry sky marshals. Yet gaps remain, as not all baggage on domestic services are screened and little cargo is inspected. For instance, some MPs still claim that today more than 22,600 aircraft carrying unscreened cargo fly into New York's airports each month. There is also a story of a man that was able to ship himself inside a box on a cargo plane from Newark to his father's home in Dallas.

Another proposal was the transmission of a manifest containing personal data on passengers and crews by all carriers operating flights to the US. This rule of conduct encountered strong resistance because it violated European privacy laws. An agreement on this point was finally reached in the last quarter of 2003, when European airlines serving the US agreed to provide to the Customs and Border Protection Bureau their passenger name records (PNRs). The data, which extends from credit card information to meal preferences, will be stored for 3 and a half years before being destroyed, rather than up to 50 years as first requested by the US. This information is being used to screen passengers for possible involvement in terrorist activities or other serious crimes.

Measures Adopted in Europe

In the meantime, an EU Council of Transport Ministers ruled out a security regulation act on December 8, 2001. This document included the application of a new package of common rules for aviation security consistent with Title 6 of the EU Treaty.

This act is composed of 10 articles only, as all details concerning security measures to be adopted are in its annexes. This document provides the constitution of one single Authority in each country to be responsible for all security issues. Second, an auditing program for the adopted measures, under the responsibility of this central security Authority, is scheduled, too.

The bundle of technical elements contained in the regulation and its annexes are not significantly different from decisions taken in the US, expect for the fact that European ones seem to be more rational. These are:

- control of airport infrastructures;

- close attention to personnel working within airports and on objects and vehicles used for their own job purposes;
- inspection and protection of parked aircraft;
- checking passengers and separation between incoming and outgoing ones (this aspect was not included in the US regulation);
- inspection of hand and belly baggage and reconciliation between passenger and baggage at boarding;
- control of mail and cargo;
- control of general aviation.

These measures were a direct consequence of the work by the three ECAC's task forces. The auditing program will have to gain the support of ECAC itself, too, as this body has the necessary expertise to apply these rules and audit programs to all 38 member countries.

ICAO Interministerial Conference, Montreal, February 19-20, 2002

This conference, which was fixed during ICAO's Board of September 2001, saw the presence of more than 700 delegates (80 of them were Transport Ministers) representing 154 countries and 24 international organisations.

The final declaration of principles of this meeting restated a strong condemnation of the use of civil aircraft as weapons of destruction while emphasizing the role that the airline business would continue to have for world economic development. At the same time, it has been ruled out that safety and security would become primary goals of civil aviation. The responsibility of single States in this field was emphasised; moreover, a path towards a common approachfor all countries was considered.

From an operational point of view, this meeting saw a strong consensus around what was called 'ICAO Aviation Security Plan of Action', the main points of which are as follows:

- identification, analysis and development of a global response to new threats, by means of measures at airports, in relation to cockpits, passengers and ATC procedures;
- protection of cockpit doors, by reinforcing ICAO security norms;
- mandatory and periodical audits to assure security measures are being put into practice by member States in a similar and consistent way and under the control of ICAO;
- technical assistance to States that need it;

- reinforcement of the AVSEC (Aviation Security) mechanism by a voluntary additional financing of up to 15 million USD. Many States agreed to give this additional money, the first being the United States.

In this meeting, an information paper produced by the Uzbekistan delegation was presented and judged to be of particular interest by all delegates. The Asian country proposed the development of an international database of 'most-wanted people'. This database could be created by linking CRS (Computer Reservation System) information with national police, Interpol and security agencies. From many quarters it was argued that this idea could become one of the best solutions for fighting the terrorist threat.

Initial Economic Effects of the Increase in Security Measures

It's difficult not to admit that measures taken up until now might create distortions in the mechanism of competitive regulation. For instance, many Third-World countries have not provided any economic support to their local airlines. The EU has strongly opposed the US Government's continued practice of providing economic subsidies to national carriers, as claiming that they have used this money to slash fares on transatlantic routes to mainland Europe.

Therefore, the XXXII Assembly of September 2001 has adopted Resolution A33-20 that urges coordination between member States in the assistance practices to the air transport industry. The same Assembly has also formed a special group of experts in the field of war risk.

All over the world there has been a general consensus towards a reduction of expenses on non-core investments. However, while some airports and service providers (especially in Europe and North America) have cut their fares to arrest the decline in movements, Pacific Rim airports have actually raised charges for take-off, landing and parking rights.

Another significant point refers to the fact that the strong pressure that air transport is being faced with due to the combined effects of traffic decrease and cost duplication has lead many States to partly break away from local deregulation processes. In this sense, 2004, with traffic figures hopefully coming back to pre-2001 levels, should mark a cornerstone and push towards new challenges in the macro-environmental area, as in the case of the EU-USA negotiations for a final agreement about a common 'Open Skies' regime.

The Economic Condition of the Air Transport Industry

The tragic events of September 2001 simply exacerbated a condition of structural crisis that most carriers were already facing. In some cases, this position has been exploited to obtain easier state aids or to implement long awaited reengineering turnarounds under Chapter 11's regime.

In the period between 1990 and 2000, the US environment has seen a huge entry of new start-up carriers, some of which have later gone into bankruptcy or been acquired by other players. Today in this market we can count 7 major airlines and 40 regional players.

Even in the European context, and most definitely in the EU case, a younger liberalisation process encouraged dozens of new start-ups to enter the market and start bloody fare wars with incumbents. This has deeply impacted on flag carriers' rent-positions, that have been economically supported for many decades by their respective member States and now in the deregulated scenario, at least theoretically, can no longer receive assistance.

However, the main difference between the US and the EU lies in the fact that in the latter's case the incumbents' capacity does not disappear even if the carrier fails. A clear example of this is provided by the recent Swissair and Sabena bankruptcies, these carriers striking back again with different names (Swiss and SN Brussels Airlines) but with most of their past strategic weaknesses. The recent announcements concerning the KLM-Air France merger, and negotiations under way for integration between Iberia and British Airways, should get a green light within 2004 and probably, provide some relief to a European sector which still suffers from deep fragmentation of market shares.

To promote consolidation, the EU could also study the introduction of some tax incentive, for instance. The final goal should be to have no more than 4 major airlines and 20 regional ones in Europe: today, instead, there are 20 relatively large operators and 50 regionals in the industry.

New security measures, such as the ones mentioned above, may in fact have some negative effects both on the total number of passengers and on the time involved in boarding procedures. Traffic decreases after September 11 has reduced cases of delays; but, when the demand jumps back, these problems will occur again. But, most of all, these measures could also become a new heavy burden on airlines' operating costs. Giovanni Bisignani, director general and CEO of IATA recently said that a 7-8% bounce-back in international revenue passenger kilometres is expected in 2004, but that the latest security developments could put that growth in jeopardy. Other analysts claim that security incidents will have an effect on the traffic and financial results for the first quarter of 2004, which is usually one of the weakest of the year. But if the higher levels of security and flight cancellations continue into the second and third quarters, usually the best of the year, the impact on 2004 results could be pretty devastating.

In the case of airports, it's common knowledge that, above a certain level of traffic, the aviation-related activity is able to produce positive net margins of around 10%. Airport enterprises, however, are being charged for most of the new security-related costs. For instance, the purchase of X-Ray machines for 100% baggage screening could cost up to 20 million Euros in the case of airports with 20-30 million passengers per year. In this sense, the question concerning who really is going to pay for these costs, whether it is the State, airports, or passengers, is leading to different answers from one country to another. Airport Council International (ACI) has made its view clear. As the primary targets of this new form of terrorist attacks are States, and not airlines or airports, it is States which should pay all increased security-related costs.

According to these factors, the air transport scenario presents a condition of deep turmoil that will soon drive to a revision of the current market boundaries. This change will be accelerated, in the case of the European environment, by extraordinary finance operations and alliances policies to increase its competitiveness.

This radical turnaround appears urgent in the case of network-based 'grandfather carriers' that are now being faced with the threat of low-cost operators. The latter seem to have adopted a winning strategy that better adheres to the type of demand and psychology of the modern passenger. Airports, too, will have to find new paths to cope with privatisation processes, the end of public financing of infrastructural upgrades, and will need to establish different market relationships with airlines.

Thus, the consequences of September 11 do not have to be confined only to security fields, but will involve all economic aspects of the air transport value chain in the next few years.

Moreover, the 'Twin Towers effect' has also shown a socio-political problem that Western countries will soon have to face in any case in a serious attempt. This is very easy to be enucleated: the existence of significant gaps in lifestyle conditions between wealthy and poor countries will continue to be a rich breeding ground around which terrorism will grow and punish the weaknesses of Western economies.

This long-lasting macro problem, of course, requires a supranational cooperative strategy that involves intergovernmental coordination and not solely industry practices within the air transport value chain.

Chapter 9

The Airport Industry: An International Picture

The Airport Business in 2002

The Airport Council International (ACI) statistics for 2002 show little change from previous year.

A positive note came from the last months of the year, which saw some stability returning to the market. In fact, the declines in passenger numbers had been largely levelled out during the third quarter and, in December, passenger traffic was up by 12%, while both cargo and aircraft movements were up when compared with December of the previous year. Table 9.1 illustrates the top 40 airports in the world for passenger movements, while table 9.22 provides evidence concerning the top 10 cargo airports.

US Performance in 2002

Despite all the industry's problems, American airports held on to no less than five of the world's top ten positions, although only Atlanta actually scored an increase in passenger movements.

It must also be remembered that 2002 saw some of the US majors come close to total collapse and the airport industry takes comfort from their survival to date.

In the future, loss of hub status by some airports, like Philadelphia or Charlotte, could lead to stronger shakeouts in market shares and overall movements by the main US airport players. On the contrary, performances registered at New York's JFK by low-cost carriers, notably Jet Blue, show what can be achieved when you put the right product in a good catchment area. Table 9.3 shows figures concerning America's top ten airports for passenger movements.

Table 9.1 Top 40 world airports in 2002 (passenger movements)

Rank 2002	Rank 2001	Airport city	Total pax.	% Chg.
1	1	Atlanta (ATL)	76,876,128	1.3
2	2	Chicago (ORD)	66,565,952	(1.3)
3	4	London (LHR)	63,338,641	4.3
4	5	Tokyo (HND)	61,079,478	4.1
5	3	Los Angeles (LAX)	56,223,843	(8.7)
6	6	Dallas (DFW)	52,828,573	(4.2)
7	7	Frankfurt (FRA)	48,450,357	(0.2)
8	8	Paris (CDG)	48,350,172	0.7
9	9	Amsterdam (AMS)	40,736,009	3.0
10	10	Denver (DEN)	35,651,098	(1.2)
11	11	Phoenix (PHX)	35,547,167	0.3
12	12	Las Vegas (LAS)	35,009,011	(0.5)
13	16	Madrid (MAD)	33,913,456	(0.4)
14	14	Houston (IAH)	33,905,253	(2.6)
15	17	Hong Kong (HKG)	33,882,463	4.1
16	13	Minneapolis (MSP)	32,628,331	(3.3)
17	18	Detroit (DTW)	32,477,694	(0.5)
18	21	Bangkok (BKK)	32,182,980	5.1
19	15	San Francisco (SFO)	31,456,422	(9.2)
20	19	Miami (MIA)	30,060,241	(5.1)
21	23	New York (JFK)	29,943,084	2.0
22	20	London (LGW)	29,628,423	(5.0)
23	22	Newark (EWR)	29,202,654	(6.1)
24	25	Singapore (SIN)	28,979,344	3.2
25	30	Tokyo (NRT)	28,883,606	13.8
26	33	Beijing (PEK)	27,159,665	12.3
27	27	Seattle (SEA)	26,690,843	(1.3)
28	24	Orlando (MCO)	26,653,672	(5.7)
29	26	Toronto (YYZ)	25,930,363	(7.5)
30	28	St.Louis (STL)	25,626,114	(3.9)
31	29	Rome (FCO)	25,340,383	(0.9)
32	34	Philadelphia (PHL)	24,799,470	1.0
33	36	Charlotte (CLT)	23,597,926	1.8
34	37	Paris (ORY)	23,169,725	0.6
35	35	Munich (MUC)	23,163,720	(2.0)
36	31	Sydney (SYD)	22.797.724	(7.9)
37	37	Boston (BOS)	22,696,141	(7.3)
38	39	New York (LGA)	21,986,679	(2.4)
39	42	Barcelona (BCN)	21,345,090	2.9
40	66	Seoul (ICN)	21,057,093	44.4

Source: ACI data.

Table 9.2 Top 10 world airports in 2002 (cargo movements)

Rank	Airport City	Total cargo	% Chg.
1	Memphis (MEM)	3,390,800	28.8
2	Hong Kong (HKG)	2,504,584	19.3
3	Tokyo (NRT)	2,001,822	19.1
4	Los Angeles (LAX)	1,779,855	0.3
5	Anchorage (ANC)	1,771,595	(5.5)
6	Seoul (ICN)	1,705,880	43.2
7	Singapore (SIN)	1,660,404	8.5
8	Frankfurt (FRA)	1,631,322	1.1
9	Paris (CDG)	1,626,400	2.2
10	Miami (MIA)	1,624,242	(0.9)

Source: ACI data.

European Performances in 2002

Positions in the rankings for 2002 remained stable, with London Heathrow scoring a significant 4.3% increase in a very tough year and Paris CDG and Frankfurt retaining their second and third place, although with slightly decreasing passenger traffic.

Even in the European environment the low-cost revolution proved to be a market bonanza for many secondary airports, with London Stansted probably being the best example to date.

Table 9.4 shows the ten best traffic records for 2002 in the European context.

Table 9.3 Top 10 airports in the USA, 2002 (passenger movements)

Rank	Airport City	Total Pax.	% Chg.
1	Atlanta (ATL)	76,876,128	1.3
2	Chicago (ORD)	66,565,952	(1.3)
3	Los Angeles (LAX)	56,223,843	(4.2)
4	Dallas/Ft.Worth (DFW)	52,828,573	(4.2)
5	Denver (DEN)	35,651,098	(1.2)
6	Phoenix (PHX)	35,547,167	0.3
7	Las Vegas (LAS)	35,009,011	(0.5)
8	Houston (IAH)	33,905,253	(2.6)
9	Minneapolis/St.Paul (MSP)	32,628,331	(3.3)
10	Detroit (DTW)	32,477,694	(0.5)

Source: ACI data.

Table 9.4 Top 10 European airports in 2002 (passenger movements)

Rank	Airport City	Total Pax.	% Chg.
1	London/Heathrow (LHR)	63,338,641	4.3
2	Frankfurt (FRA)	48,450,357	(0.2)
3	Paris (CDG)	48,350,172	0.7
4	Amsterdam (AMS)	40,736,009	3.0
5	Madrid (MAD)	33,913,456	(0.4)
6	London/Gatwick (LGW)	29,628,423	(5.0)
7	Rome (FCO)	25,340,383	(0.9)
8	Paris/Orly (ORY)	23,169,725	0.6
9	Munich (MUC)	23,163,720	(2.0)
10	Barcelona (BCN)	21,345,090	2.9

Source: ACI data.

Asia/Pacific Performance in 2002

Tokyo Haneda, acting primarily as a domestic airport in the Japanese market, was the leader for the Asia/Pacific area, with traffic figures exceeding those of Hong Kong and Bangkok combined.

A significant year-on-year increase came from the completion of traffic transfer from Kimpo to the new Incheon airport in Seoul. The overall growth in traffic records for 2002, thanks to a lesser impact of September 11 effects on this region, will probably reverse figures in 2003, due to the outbreak of the SARS.

Table 9.5 illustrates the top 10 performers in the Asia/Pacific region for 2002.

Table 9.5 Top 10 airports in the Asian/Pacific environment, 2002 (passenger movements)

Rank	Airport	Total Pax.	% Chg.
1	Tokyo/Haneda (HND)	61,079,478	4.1
2	Hong Kong (HKG)	33,882,463	4.1
3	Bangkok (BKK)	32,182,980	5.1
4	Singapore (SIN)	28,979,344	3.2
5	Tokyo/Narita (NRT)	28,883,606	13.8
6	Beijing (PEK)	27,159,665	12.3
7	Sydney (SYD)	22,797,724	(7.9)
8	Seoul/Incheon (ICN)	21,057,093	44.4
9	Fukuoka (FUK)	19,523,495	(0.3)
10	Taipei (TPE)	19,228,411	4.2

Source: ACI data.

Middle East/Africa In 2002

The scene here is dominated by Dubai airport, with Johannesburg in second place . Saudi Arabia's two largest airports – Jeddah and Riyadh – follow at a distance, with Cairo being stable in fifth position.

Overall, the region recorded a good increase in traffic movements, strongest in the Middle Eastern area, thanks to some innovative actions to promote these countries as a tourist destination.

Table 9.6, completes the description of Middle Eastern/African airports.

Table 9.6 Middle East and Africa figures, 2002

Rank	Airport City	Total Pax.	% Chg.
1	Dubaï (DXB)	15,973,391	18.3
2	Johannesburg (JNB)	12,743,545	8.1
3	Jeddah (JED)	10,945,192	5.6
4	Riyadh (RUH)	9,425,420	3.7
5	Cairo (CAI)	8,932,670	0.9
6	Algiers (ALG)	4,294,893	8.4
7	Kuwait (KWI)	4,265,044	8.6
8	Manama (BAH)	4,147,105	3.9
9	Abu Dhabi (AUH)	3,972,897	10.7
10	Casablanca (CMB)	3,449,225	(1.9)

Source : ACI data.

The Airport Business in 2003

Last year started reasonably well for most carriers. However, the combined mix of the war in Iraq, the SARS epidemic and ongoing security concerns meant that by mid-year traffic levels had been hit hard.

The impact of SARS has proved to be particularly damaging to the airport business. Asia, the only market that had been partly exempt from previous negative waves, like the US recession, September 11 and the Afghanistan war, has been deeply effected by SARS. For instance, Singapore Airlines and Cathay Pacific have been forced to ground around 40% of their capacity, even after a tremendous effort in terms of price cuttings to maintain decent loads.

Negative consequences for Asian hubs are evident, too, especially Singapore, Hong Kong and Chinese hubs, with many airport players forced to cut their charges to prevent major traffic losses.

Only in the last quarter of 2003, have signs of recovery been visible, this result being reached even though the Japanese market has remained weak and yields have not yet returned to pre-SARS levels at year end. Nevertheless, cargo has continued to grow despite the downturn and IATA expects international cargo traffic to show a 5% rise for 2003.

Table 9.7, 9.8 and 9.9 provide data concerning the top 30 world airports in 2003.

Table 9.7 Top 30 world airports in 2003 (passenger movements)

Airport	Passengers 2003	Delta % 2003/2002
Atlanta (ATL)	79,086,792	2.9
Chicago (ORD)	69,354,154	4.2
London (LHR)	63,468,620	0.2
Tokyo (HND)	63,172,925	3.4
Los Angeles (LAX)	54,969,053	(2.2)
Dallas (DFW)	53,243,061	0.8
Frankfurt (FRA)	48,351,664	(0.2)
Paris (CDG)	48,122,038	(0.4)
Amsterdam (AMS)	39,959,161	(1.9)
Denver (DEN)	37,462,428	5.1
Phoenix (PHX)	37,409,388	5.2
Las Vegas (LAS)	36,265,705	3.6
Madrid (MAD)	35,694,331	5.2
Houston (IAH)	34,119,680	0.6
Minneapolis (MSP)	33,195,873	2.0
Detroit (DTW)	32,679,350	0.2
New York (JFK)	31,712,728	5.0
Bangkok (BKK)	30,175,379	(6.2)
London (LGW)	30,007,209	1.3
Miami (MIA)	29,595,618	(1.5)
Newark (EWR)	29,584,600	1.2
San Francisco (SFO)	29,296,681	(6.8)
Orlando (MCO)	27,316,221	2.5
Hong Kong (HKG)	26,774,000	(21)
Seattle (SEA)	26,752,768	0.2
Tokyo (NRT)	26,492,384	(8.3)
Rome (FCO)	26,285,036	3.7
Toronto (YYZ)	24,739,784	(4.6)
Sydney (SYD)	24,704,132	4.8
Philadelphia (PHL)	24,671,074	(0.5)

Source: ACI data.

Table 9.8 Top 30 world airports in 2003 (cargo movements)

Airport	Cargo ton	Delta % 2003/2002
Memphis (MEM)	3,390,515	0
Hong Kong (HKG)	2,668,624	6.5
Tokyo (NRT)	2,147,212	7.3
Anchorage (ANC)	2,097,488	2.7
Seoul (ICN)	1,843,054	8
Los Angeles (LAX)	1,806,164	2.7
Frankfurt (FRA)	1,650,599	1.2
Miami (MIA)	1,637,278	0.8
New York (JFK)	1,633,026	2.9
Singapore (SIN)	1,632,409	(1.7)
Louisville (SDF)	1,617,907	6.2
Chicago (ORD)	1,604,755	23.7
Taipei (TPE)	1,500,071	8.6
Paris (CDG)	1,481,200	5.9
Amsterdam (AMS)	1,353,729	5.1
London (LHR)	1,300,420	(0.8)
Shanghai (IUG)	1,189,307	87.3
Dubai (DXB)	956,845	21.9
Bangkok (BKK)	950,487	(0.7)
Indianapolis (IND)	890,615	2.8
Newark (EWR)	868,164	1
Atlanta (ATL)	797,419	8.6
Osaka (KIX)	793,476	(1.5)
Tokyo (HND)	722,533	2.2
Dallas (DFW)	667,527	(0.3)
Beijing (PEK)	662,141	(0.9)
Luxemburg (LUX)	642,995	10.8
Oakland (OAK)	619,802	(4.7)
Kuala Lumpur (KUL)	589,996	12.8
Brussels (BRU)	578,865	13.2

Source: ACI data.

Table 9.9 Top 30 world airports in 2003 (aircraft movements)

Airport	Aircraft Movements	Delta % 2003/2002
Chicago (ORD)	928,889	(0.2)
Atlanta (ATL)	911,723	2.4
Dallas (DFW)	765,296	0
Los Angeles (LAX)	622,378	(3.6)
Phoenix (PHX)	541,771	(0.7)
Paris (CDG)	515,025	1
Minneapolis (MSP)	512,267	0.9
Cincinnati (CWG)	505,557	3.9
Las Vegas (LAS)	501,029	0.8
Denver (DEN)	497,202	0.6
Detroit (DTW)	491,045	(1.2)
Houston (IAH)	474,913	4
London (LHR)	463,650	(0.6)
Los Angeles (VNY)	460,734	(7.6)
Frankfurt (FRA)	458,865	0.1
Philadelphia (PHL)	446,529	(4.8)
Charlotte (CLT)	441,246	(3.1)
Miami (MIA)	417,423	(6.5)
Amsterdam (AMS)	408,297	(2.1)
Newark (EWR)	404,596	(0.3)
Memphis (MEM)	402,258	0.9
Salt Lake City (SLC)	400,452	(1.6)
Phoenix (DVT)	388,669	0.1
Sanford (SFB)	385,303	3.2
Madrid (MAD)	388,799	4.3
St. Louis (STL)	379,772	(13.1)
New York (LGA)	374,450	3.3
Boston (BOS)	373,251	(4.8)
Toronto (YYZ)	370,866	(3.2)
Pittsburgh (PIT)	361,329	(15)

Source: ACI data.

2005 Outlook for the Air Transport Industry

IATA and ICAO both predict a steady recovery in traffic for 2005, following the positive path of 2004. IATA is expecting a bounce-back of 7-8% for international passenger traffic, with Asia leading the way. ICAO says that overall traffic is expected to increase by about 4% at a rate of 5% from 2005 and beyond. On the other hand, cargo traffic should grow by just under 4% on last year. Table 9.10 illustrates the top 30 airports in 2004 in terms of passenger numbers.

Airbus and Boeing's predictions are also consistent with those provided by international bodies. Although they do not expect orders to pick up again until 2005, the worst of the descent from the peak in 2000 appears to be over. One of the greatest threats, however, now lies in the drastic increase in fuel prices, that can negatively impact on the industry's speed of recovery.

Table 9.10 Top 30 world airports in 2004 (passenger movements)

Rank	City (Airport)	Total Passengers	% Change 2004-2003
1	Atlanta (ATL)	83,578,906	5.7
2	Chicago (ORD)	75,373,888	7.1
3	London (LHR)	67,343,960	6.1
4	Tokyo (HND)	62,320,968	(0.9)
5	Los Angeles (LAX)	60,710,830	10.4
6	Dallas/Ft.Worth (DFW)	59,412,217	11.6
7	Frankfurt (FRA)	51,098,271	5.7
8	Paris (CDG)	50,860,561	5.5
9	Amsterdam (AMS)	42,541,180	6.5
10	Denver (DEN)	42,393,693	13
11	Las Vegas (LAS)	41,436,571	14.3
12	Phoenix (PHX)	39,493,519	5.5
13	Madrid (MAD)	38,525,899	7.5
14	Bangkok (BKK)	37,960,169	25.8
15	New York (JFK)	37,362,010	17.7
16	Minneapolis/St.Paul (MSP)	36,748,577	10.7
17	Hong Kong (HKG)	36,713,000	36.1
18	Houston (IAH)	36,490,828	6.8
19	Detroit (DTW)	35,199,307	7.8
20	Beijing (PEK)	34,833,190	43.2
21	San Francisco (SFO)	33,497,084	14.3
22	Newark (EWR)	31,847,280	8.1
23	London (LGW)	31,461,523	4.8
24	Orlando (MCO)	31,110,852	13.9
25	Tokyo (NRT)	31,106,264	17.2
26	Singapore (SIN)	30,353,565	23.1
27	Miami (MIA)	30,156,727	1.9
28	Seattle/ Tacoma (SEA)	28,703,352	7.2
29	Toronto (YYZ)	28,655,526	15.8
30	Philadelphia (PHL)	28,508,510	15.6

Source: ACI data.

Afterword

Airlines need airports to operate from, while airports need airlines for their future development. This is common sense, but it also implies close links between airlines and airport authorities.

Needless to say day-to-day cooperation is essential in the field of operations. This also applies to passenger handling, safety and security concerns, environmental issues, and recreation areas. Airports want efficient use of their infrastructure, while airlines want smooth passenger flows. Both, however, are seeking to meet passenger expectations at the same time as obtaining a profitable return on their investment. Consequently, for optimum operations, common basic views have to be worked out in the planning phases.

Both airport and airline activities require huge investments and long lead times, particularly when they concern aircraft and airport infrastructure. This implies very long-range planning, which is a highly critical factor in the air transport business. Accurate forecasting is necessary, as this business is highly dependent on the global economic situation. Both airlines and airports sometimes have to look beyond the current downturn and secure adequate investments with a view to future growth. On the other hand, in an upturn, they have to be careful not to be over optimistic in their long-term commitments. It is therefore very useful for airport authorities and the airlines operating at their airports to share a minimum amount of long-term planning information. There is no future for an ambitious airport development program which is not consistent with a similar long-term airline development program, and this works both ways.

Once the long-term planning phase is over, it is time to start designing future processes for passenger flows, aircraft handling, and all other operational sectors. A very delicate coordination process between the airport and airlines involved has to be set up. Each party has to understand the other's strategy in order to ensure consistency between infrastructure design constraints, smooth passenger handling, airline ground operation requirements, and individual investment limitations. In addition, there has to be a clear understanding of projected regulatory constraints, mainly concerning security and safety processes, by all the parties involved.

The relationship between airlines and airports has always been driven by three main factors. Firstly, local air transport market potential, either for inbound or outbound traffic, secondly the size of the airport - is it intended to become a main hub, a significant gateway or a regional airport? - and finally the situation of the airline involved – is it a strong member of a global alliance, a sizeable point-to-point operator or a niche airline? Large alliance members regularly look to small viable regional airports to feed their hubs, while niche operators often have their say in the organization of large hubs as the increasing number of small flows generates profitable margins. So each of the partners in this business has to figure out what the strategies of the other players are. Their own strategy cannot be fully independent. Managing the smallest airport requires an efficient survey of local markets, as it is necessary to identify what its future could be with local airlines and any alliances and hubs it may be in a position to operate with.

In addition, there has always been a temptation for the airport community to slowly move into non-air transport businesses: shops, restaurants, theaters, business centers. There is no doubt that these activities generate additional revenues for airports. However, they very often create tension among airlines operating at this airport and the airport authorities concerned, as the former consider that these activities take up a significant amount of space which would normally be dedicated to the core business, i.e. the handling of passengers and cargo. In this respect, compromises are still pretty hard to reach, but are necessary to deal with each individual case, or at least to achieve a proper balance between investment returns and operational requirements.

In the last few years, three more factors have taken on considerable importance and have forced airlines to move into more in-depth cooperation: alternate ground transportation modes, environmental pressures and security processes.

For almost two decades, after having improved highway networks, Western Europe, and particularly France, has steadily evolved towards major high-speed train infrastructures. This factor cannot be ignored when talking about air transport strategy. It will have more influence on the profitability of some point-to-point air traffic, small regional airports, and also on some of the decisions taken by major airlines, who will be looking into inter-modal processes, and big airports, which will have to accommodate railway stations as an integral part of their infrastructure plans.

All over the world, local communities have always benefited from the air transport business – airlines and airports – through the job opportunities they bring. On the other hand, these same communities have also become a powerful influence in environmental issues. There is no viable future in any airport if the airlines and airport authorities involved do not jointly address environmental issues. This requires using new technological enhancements developed by aircraft and engine manufacturers, and also very close technical cooperation to design new descent and climb procedures to address noise path problems. It also requires a comprehensive joint public relations policy to explain and promote the environmental improvements and benefits in terms of job opportunities for the communities.

Following closely behind flight safety, which is now taken for granted, security will definitely become the main common concern of both airports and airlines. Additional tougher procedures have recently been introduced, and will be supplemented in the future to ensure the ongoing improvement of security standards. This is a very serious matter that cannot be addressed without a common understanding of all aspects of security. In the medium term, significant progress will have to be made and publicized in order to raise confidence among passengers and local communities. In the long run, it goes without saying that security matters will have a great influence on the design of future premises and on passenger, baggage and cargo flow processes. Both airports and airlines will have to rapidly work out enhancements that will ease passenger flows, otherwise the future of air transport might be in jeopardy.

Managing air transport businesses necessarily leads to compromises involving a delicate combination of so-called hard factors (mainly areas of concern for airport authorities) and so-called soft factors representing the airlines' strategy. These are compounded by the prospects for alternative ground transportation modes, local communities' wishes with respect to jobs and environmental issues, and deep-rooted security concerns. Airlines and airports are obliged to work together very closely, from the very early planning stages right up to day-to-day operations. The range of contacts also means anything from one-to-one relationships to encompassing the needs of all the players involved.

From the customers' point of view, closer cooperation will be increasingly necessary for the simple reason that if customers don't have a good perception of the situation with regard to airport infrastructure or airline operations, it will obviously impact on the image of both partners.

Nowadays, particularly in the air transport business, prosperity and strong economic and operating performance go hand in hand with a good image.

There is no future for head-to-head opposition between airlines and airports. Success and profitable growth very much depend on the way the two parties meet the challenges together.

Jean Cyrill Spinetta
Chairman IATA and Air France

Bibliography

Berry, L. (1986), 'Big ideas in Services Management', *Journal of Consumer Marketing*, pp. 47-51.

Caves, R. and Gosling, G. (1999), *Strategic Airport Planning*, Pergamon, London.

D'Aveni, R. (1994), *Hypercompetition*, Free Press, New York.

Doganis, R. (1992), *The Airport Business*, Routledge, London.

Doganis, R. (2001), *The Airine Business in the Twenty-first Century*, Routledge, London.

Doz, Y. and Hamel, G. (1998), *Alliance Advantage: The Art of Creating Value through Partnering*, Harvard Business School Press, Cambridge.

Graham, A. (2001), *Managing airports*, Butterworth Heinemann, Oxford.

Hamel G. (2000), *Leading the Revolution*, Harvard Business School Press, Cambridge.

Hanlon, P. (1996), *Global airlines: competition in a transnational industry*, Butterworth Heinemann, London.

Holloway, S. (2003), *Straight and Level: Practical Airline Economics*, 2nd edition, Ashgate Publishing, Aldershot.

Humphries, G. (1996), *The Future of Airport Retailing*, Financial Times Management Reports, London.

Ionides, N. and O'Connell, J. (2004), 'Room for all?', *Airline Business*, April, pp. 30-32.

Jarach, D. (1998), 'Alliances in the airline market: an empirical perspective', *Proceedings of the 33rd Annual CTRF Conference*, University of Saskatoon, Saskatchewan Press, Saskatchewan, pp. 315-330.

Jarach, D. (1999), 'La reingegnerizzazione dell'offerta logistica: la logica dei network hub & spokes', *Commercio* 64, pp. 125-140.

Jarach, D. (2001), 'The evolution of airport management practices: towards a multi-point, multi-service, marketing-driven firm', *Journal of Air Transport Management*, 7, pp. 119-125.

Jarach, D. (2002), *Marketing Aeroportuale*, EGEA, Milan.

Jarach, D. (2004), 'Future scenarios for the European airline industry: a marketing-based perspective', *Journal of Air Transportation*, forthcoming.

Kotler, P. and Scott, W. (1997), *Marketing Management*, Italian edition, ISEDI, Turin.

Levitt, T. (1969), *The Marketing Mode*, McGraw Hill, New York.

Levitt, T. (1980), 'Marketing success through differentiation – of anything', *Harvard Business Review*, January-February, pp. 83-91.

Lovelock, C. (1984), *Services Marketing*, Prentice Hall, Englewood Cliffs.

Morrison, S. and Winston, C. (1995), *The evolution of the airline industry*, The Brookings Institution, Washington.

Pilling, M. (2003), 'Smarter Service', *Airline Business*, January, pp. 36-39.

Pilling, M. (2003), 'Seeking Stability', *Airline Business*, January, p. 41.
Pilling, M. (2003), 'Terms of Engagement', *Airline Business*, December, p. 46.
Pilling, M. and Pinkham, R. (2003), 'Flight support', *Airline Business*, October, pp. 63-67.
Pilling, M. and Field D. (2004), 'Community Spirit', *Airline Business*, April, pp. 62-64.
Pralahad, C.K. and Ramaswamy, V. (2004), *The future of competition: co-creating unique value with customers*, Harvard Business School Press, Cambridge.
Shaw, S. (1999), *Airline Marketing and Management*, Ashgate Publishing, Aldershot.
Sparaco, P. and Barrie, D. (2004), 'Marshal Law', *Aviation Week & Space Technology*, January 12, pp. 35-36.
Taneja, N. (2003), *Airline Survival Kit*, Ashgate Publishing, Aldershot.
Valdani, E. and Jarach, D. (1996), 'La deregulation del trasporto aereo in Europa: il caso Italia', *Economia & Management*, 5, pp. 89-99.
Valdani, E. and Jarach, D. (1997), *Compagnie aeree e deregulation, strategie di marketing nei cieli senza frontiere*, EGEA, Milan.

Index

3M